Cyclopedia of
Young Adult Authors

Cyclopedia of
Young Adult Authors

Volume 2

C. S. Forester–Joan Lowery Nixon

From
The Editors of Salem Press

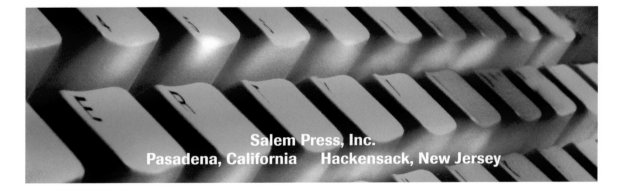

Salem Press, Inc.
Pasadena, California   Hackensack, New Jersey

Editor in Chief: Dawn P. Dawson

Project Editors: Kenneth T. Burles
R. Kent Rasmussen

Acquisitions Editor: Mark Rehn

Production Editor: Cynthia Beres

Photograph Editor: Philip Bader

Design: Moritz Design, Pasadena, California

Page Layout and Graphics: James Hutson

Assistant Editor: Andrea E. Miller

Editorial Intern: Heather Pistole

Library of Congress Cataloging-in-Publication Data

Cyclopedia of young adult authors / from the editors of Salem Press.
p. cm.
Includes bibliographical references and index.
ISBN 1-58765-206-4 (set : alk. paper) — ISBN 1-58765-207-2 (vol. 1 : alk. paper) —
ISBN 1-58765-208-0 (vol. 2 : alk. paper) — ISBN 1-58765-209-9 (vol. 3 : alk. paper)
1. Young adult literature, American—Dictionaries. 2. Young adult literature, English—
Dictionaries. 3. Authors, American—Biography—Dictionaries. 4. Authors, English—
Biography—Dictionaries. I. Salem Press.
PS490.C93 2005
810.9'9283'03—dc22

2004027668

First Printing
Printed in Canada

Contents

Volume 2

Cyclopedia of
Young Adult Authors

C. S. Forester

Born: August 27, 1899; Cairo, Egypt
Died: April 2, 1966; Fullerton, California

www.csforester.org

In British naval officer Horatio Hornblower, **C. S. Forester** created one of the most famous characters in modern fiction. Eleven books trace Hornblower's career from a lowly midshipman in the late eighteenth century to an admiral. Hornblower goes from one brilliant triumph to another, but despite his great successes, he is a highly introspective character ever burdened with the fear that failure, ruin, and even death may be just around the corner.

English by his parentage, Forester was born Cecil Lewis Troughton Smith in Egypt, where his father was a teacher. At an early age, he went to England with his mother and siblings. There he grew up as a bookish child who excelled in school. A passionate reader, he was especially interested in military history, so it is not surprising that most of the fiction he later wrote is set in military conflicts. He entered adolescence as World War I was slaughtering the young men of his generation, but he was rejected for military service because of his poor eyesight. He entered medical school in London but was set on becoming a writer. He soon abandoned his studies and began writing novels. His early efforts were all rejected, but he had some success with historical biographies. As his writing improved, he returned to novels. By the mid-1930's, he could count himself a success. Only then did he begin his Hornblower stories.

Forester wrote his first Hornblower novel after returning to England from California, where he briefly worked as a screenwriter. While sailing past

TITLES

Brown on Resolution, 1929

The African Queen, 1935

The Captain from Connecticut, 1941

Randall and the River of Time, 1950

Hornblower novels:

Mr. Midshipman Hornblower, 1950

Lieutenant Hornblower, 1952

Hornblower and the Hotspur, 1962

Hornblower and the Atropos, 1953

Beat to Quarters, 1937 (publ. in England as *The Happy Return*)

Ship of the Line, 1938

Flying Colours, 1939

Commodore Hornblower, 1945 (publ. in England as *The Commodore*)

Lord Hornblower, 1946

Admiral Hornblower in the West Indies, 1958

Hornblower and the Crisis, 1967

p.656

the wild coastline of Central America, he imagined what it might have been like in the early nineteenth century if an isolated madman there had defied Spanish rule by launching a rebellion. He then imagined that rebel leader pitted against a resourceful British naval captain, and Hornblower was born. In *Beat to Quarters* Hornblower sails to Central America in a frigate to deliver arms to rebels to force Spain to divert military resources away from Europe, where it is allied with Britain's main enemy, France. After Hornblower gives the mad rebel leader the British guns and hands over a powerful Spanish warship that his own ship captures, he learns that Spain has shifted sides. He now must fight the Spanish ship again—this time against a desperate rebel crew.

p.249

In each novel that followed, Forester gave Hornblower as much independence from higher command as possible. This allowed him to make crucial decisions on his own but also put him in positions that caused trouble with the admiralty. Much of the pleasure in reading these books comes from admiring Hornblower's ingenuity in the face of complex and rapidly changing challenges. For example, Forester's second Hornblower story, *Ship of the Line*, puts Hornblower's ship in a squadron sent into the

The African Queen

C. S. Forester was offered a Hollywood contract as a screenwriter in 1932. He spent thirteen weeks each year until 1939 in California working on film scripts. However, the most famous filmed version of Forester's work was written by director John Huston (with writer James Agee), who also directed *The African Queen* (1951). Forester had told Huston that he was never happy with the ending of the book, and as is often the case in Hollywood, Huston concluded the final episode with a happy ending. The film was nominated for many Academy Awards and earned Humphrey Bogart the Best Actor award (1951). His co-star, actress Katherine Hepburn was nominated for Best Actress in the same film.

Frigate

Navies called ships of the highest rating "ships of the line," because they were powerful enough to fight in the line of battle. "Frigates" were developed as lesser-rated ships in the eighteenth and nineteenth centuries. They were smaller ships and were used to scout for enemy fleets, to attack and defend commerce, and to carry messages and repeat flag signals from senior commanders to subordinates. Frigates carried between thirty and fifty guns firing eighteen to twenty-four pound shot.

Mediterranean but lets Hornblower seize every possible chance for independent action. *Flying Colours* continues the story with Hornblower a prisoner whom the French want to try as a war criminal. He escapes and returns to England in spectacular fashion. Later stories elevate him to ever greater heights of success, but his self-doubts always remain.

The best way to read C. S. Forester's Hornblower novels is in the order in which they trace Hornblower's career. *Mr. Midshipman Hornblower* is a particularly satisfying book for young readers as it introduces Hornblower as a gawky teenager who seems out of place among rough older sailors. Equally enjoyable is *Lieutenant Hornblower*, which puts a still young Hornblower on a frigate bound for the **West Indies** under a mad captain. After the captain is incapacitated by a mysterious accident, Hornblower leads the ship to a great triumph by tactfully suggesting to the timid acting captain one bold plan after another.

– R. Kent Rasmussen

Paula Fox

Born: April 22, 1923; New York, New York

Most of **Paula Fox**'s young adult fiction is contemporary and realistic. Most of her protagonists p.23 deal with very real problems in the contemporary world. Fox herself faced serious problems when she was growing up and treats her fictional characters' problems in a straightforward yet sympathetic manner. Her topics range from alcoholic relatives to dying parents, including a father dying from AIDS. p.10

Fox's sole historical novel *The Slave Dancer*, which won a **Newbery Medal**, is about a New Orleans boy named Jessie Bollier. Jessie is kidnapped and taken aboard a slave ship to play the fife. He is to create music to which the slaves can dance and thus get some exercise. When the ship sinks, Jessie escapes. The book is highly controversial, with some critics arguing that its depiction of the slaves is too negative. p.10 p.251

In *A Place Apart* Fox moved to a contemporary theme: a girl whose father dies when she is thirteen. She must deal not only with her father's death but also with economic problems, a move, and her mother's interest in remarrying. *The Village by the Sea*'s central character, Emma, spends two weeks with her aunt and uncle, whom she hardly knows, while her father undergoes heart surgery. Her aunt is an alcoholic who

p.117

resents anyone else's happiness. Emma finds escape by building a model village with a friend she meets at the beach, but her aunt viciously destroys the village. *The Moonlight Man* also deals with a young girl, Catherine Ames, who has problems involving an alcoholic relative, her father. When she spends a few weeks with him during her summer vacation, she learns how irresponsible he is. She sees him at his worst, so drunk that she effectively becomes his caretaker. Nevertheless, she realizes that she still loves him.

In *One-Eyed Cat*, Ned Wallis takes an air rifle that he is not supposed to touch and one night shoots something moving that he cannot see clearly. Later he finds a wild one-eyed cat and concludes that he is responsible for shooting out its eye. Guilt haunts him throughout the book until, toward the end, he confesses his misdeed to his badly **arthritic** mother.

p.662

In *The Eagle Kite*, Liam Cormac's father has AIDS, supposedly from a tainted transfusion after an appendectomy. However, Liam knows that the blood supply has been safe for years and remembers having once seen his father embracing another man on the beach. Guessing that his father has contracted AIDS from **homo-sexual** activity, Liam must come to grips with his own an-

p.57

Fife

A fife is a small flute, held to the side of the mouth, with six to eight finger holes. It was used in military music as early as the late fifteenth century. The British Army used it until the end of the nineteenth century. In the U.S., it was popular during the Civil War, and many fife songs and ballads composed then still exist. The fife was often accompanied by a drum, and the fife and drum corps played marching songs to bolster the morale of the soldiers. The drum beat also helped marching soldiers stay in step. The shrill fife music could be heard above the sound of cannon fire.

ger and with his father's sexual orientation, illness, and death.

Paula Fox's works have won many awards. *The Moonlight Man* and *One-Eyed Cat* were selected as ***New York Times*** Notable Books, and *One-Eyed Cat* and *The Village by the Sea* were **Newbery Honor Books**. In 1987 she was awarded a **Silver Medallion** by the University of Southern Mississippi for making an outstanding contribution to the field of children's literature. Her sensitive portrayals of young adults and their problems make her works of enduring interest to young adults.

p.252

– Richard Tuerk

Silver Medallion

The Silver Medallion of the University of Southern Mississippi has been awarded each year since 1969 to an author or illustrator who has made an outstanding contribution to children's literature. Nominations are made by publishers, authors, illustrators, teachers, and librarians based on an author's entire body of work. A committee votes to select the winner. The silver medallion presented to the winner has the image of the winner on one side and a character from one of his or her books on the other. Additional silver medals are kept in the de Grummon Children's Literature Collection.

Jean Fritz

Born: November 16, 1915; Hankow, China

www.cbcbooks.org/html/jeanfritz.html

p.117
Jean Fritz is best known for her extensively researched biographies and **historical fiction**. She draws upon letters, diaries, and journals to ensure that her books are historically accurate and never invents dialogue for her characters. She approaches her subjects by researching their personalities first, and when she feels she has a grasp of the characters, she does what she terms "detective work," searching archives and visiting the places where the action took place. Her books manage to bring life and excitement to the past, while staying true to historical facts.

p.527
The only child of Christian **missionary** parents, Fritz was born in China and spent her first thirteen years there in a very international atmosphere. Her family lived in a French compound, and she attended a British school and learned to speak fluent Chinese. However, she never felt quite at home in China and relished the stories her father told her about American life. Because of these stories she felt homesick for America, although she had never been there. She began keeping a journal as a child in China, and later held several jobs that used her writing skills while she tried to get her books published. It was not until p.35 she had worked as a children's **librarian** for two years that she knew

TITLES

The Cabin Faced West, 1958

Brady, 1960

Early Thunder, 1967

George Washington's Breakfast, 1969

Homesick: My Own Story, 1982

Make Way for Sam Houston, 1986

George Washington's Mother, 1992

Bigamy

Bigamy means being married to more than one partner at the same time. In some parts of the world it is acceptable for a man to have one or more wives. It is also possible for a woman to have more than one husband, but this occurs less frequently. Because it is expensive to support more than one spouse, bigamy usually is practiced by the wealthy or powerful in countries where it is allowed. It is not legal to have more than one spouse at the same time in the U.S.

enough about children's literature to become successful at her career.

Fritz has chosen varied subjects for her biographies. She has written about George Washington, Sam Houston, Albert Schweitzer, Great Britain's King George III, Benjamin Franklin, and Christopher Columbus, among others. In the easy-to-read *George Washington's Mother*, Fritz humorously depicts the teenage future president as a victim of a nagging, overprotective mother. In *Make Way for Sam Houston*, aimed at more mature readers, Fritz chronicles the life of the famous Texan from his boyhood to his death. She does not shy away from depicting Houston's alcoholism and bigamy but also peppers the thoroughly researched biography with amusing anecdotes.

Fritz's first historical novel, *The Cabin Faced West*, is set in Pennsylvania in 1784. Its protagonist, ten-year-old Ann, finds life on the frontier lonely and joyless until George Washington comes down their road and stays for a meal. In *Brady*, set in 1830's Pennsylvania, a minister's son discovers a runaway slave hiding near his family's farm. When his father becomes ill, Brady must keep the secret of the Underground Railway station and help the slave to freedom. Set in Salem, Massachusetts in 1774, *Early Thunder* tells the story of Daniel West, the motherless son of a loyalist doctor during the Revolutionary War. As the townspeople ostracize Daniel's family for their political views, he must de-

p.101
p.254
p.233
p.255

cide for himself where his own loyalties lie. In a much lighter vein, *George Washington's Breakfast*, Fritz's most accessible work of fiction, follows a boy in his search to find out what Washington really ate for breakfast.

Jean Fritz's many writing awards include two **Boston Globe-Horn Book Awards** for nonfiction and four Boston Globe-Horn Honor Book Awards. *Homesick: My Own Story* won several awards, including the **Christopher Award**. Fritz has also received the **Regina Medal** of the Catholic Library Association, the American Library Association's **Laura Ingalls Wilder Award** for her lasting contribution to children's literature, and the New York State Library Association's **Knickerbocker Award** for Juvenile Literature.

p.747

p.45

– Mary Virginia Davis

The Underground Railroad

The Underground Railroad was a secret network of safe homes and routes by which slaves were helped to escape from the Deep South north to freedom. It is believed that parts of the Railroad, which was not a real railroad and not underground, may have been operating as early as 1786, but its peak period of operation was 1830-1860. Most runaway slaves were men, but women and children also escaped. Abolitionists hid, fed, and transported the runaway slaves. It is estimated that sixty thousand to one hundred thousand slaves escaped to freedom in the years 1800 to 1865.

Neil Gaiman

Born: November 10, 1960; Portchester, England

www.neilgaiman.com

Neil Gaiman first made his mark as a writer of graphic novels, especially the Sandman series, which were credited with lifting the genre from the level of comic books to literature. He has also written conventional prose novels. However, all his work is deeply imbued with fantastic, mythic, folkloric, gothic, and dreamlike storytelling.

Gaiman was born into an **upper-middle-class** family in the southern English county of Hampshire. As a child, he was a voracious reader and by his teenage years knew that he wanted to become a writer. He specifically wanted to write comic books. However, after graduating from school, his first literary career was as a **freelance journalist**. He credits this experience with teaching him how to write succinctly and capture dialogue on the page. Meanwhile, as he matured, he began to be dissatisfied with the comic books that he had enjoyed in his youth. In 1983 he came across the work of Alan Moore, whose writing for Marvel Comics was bringing a new depth to the genre. Gaiman began to think about ways in which he could write stories with depth and intellectual sophistication, geared toward adult readers, while presented in the graphic format of comics.

Gaiman enjoyed his first successes with *Ghastly Beyond Belief* (1985), *Violent Cases* (1987), and *Black Orchid* (1989), but it was with his Sandman series, which began to appear in 1990, that brought him recognition as a truly original talent. The Sandman, also known as Morpheus, or Dream, is one of

p.560

p.32

p.368

Anthropomorphic

Anthropomorphic describes something that has a human form or human characteristics. It can be a god or a supernatural being such as a ghost. One of the most common ways in which we use anthropomorphism is with our pets. We describe a dog's paws as its hands, we say that our cat is "talking" to us as if it understands our words, or we assume that pets think as we do. We interpret many of the things they do as if they were human.

.257
the Endless, a family of seven **anthropomorphic** representations of human experience: Dream, Desire, Despair, Destiny, Delirium, Destruction, and Death. In his ongoing adventures, the Sandman wanders the world, often on quests of some sort, often in situations that require various characters to tell their own stories (for the Sandman is also the Master of Story). In 1996 Gaiman ended the Sandman series so he could move on to write nonseries graphic novels, while also venturing into the realm of the conventional novel. In the late 1990's he moved from England to Minnesota, the home of his American wife.

Neverwhere is a **novelization** of a series Gaiman had written for television, in which, in typical p.105 **fantasy** fashion, a normal mortal becomes drawn p.87 into an Otherworld (this one existing in the sewers of London), where he must help save a young woman from assassination. *Stardust* is another Otherworld adventure, in which a young man ventures into Faerie to catch a star for the woman he wishes to marry, and in the process discovers that much more is at stake than simply a present for his girlfriend. *American Gods*, written for a mature reading audience, sets the old gods who accompanied immigrants to America against the gods of the postmodern world—gods

of the Internet, television, credit cards, and so on. *Coraline*, for a younger audience, tells the story of a little girl who finds herself in an alternate universe in which some things are much nicer and more exciting than her mundane life, but which also holds dangers that she must outwit.

Neil Gaiman has always prided himself on his use of folklore, mythology, and history in his stories, making great efforts to be sure that he is true to the actual stories and events even as he twists them into fantasy. It is this sense of authenticity that has won him such an enthusiastic set of readers. He has also received several major literary awards. *Stardust* p.258 was honored with the **Alex Award** of the Young Adult Library Services Association and recognition by the **American Library Association** as one of p.45 the **Best Books for Young Adults** of its year—an p.480 award that Gaiman also received for *Coraline*.

– Leslie Ellen Jones

The Alex Award

The Alex Award, first presented in 1998, honors ten books each year that were written for adult readers but are appealing to young adults (ages 12-18). The award is given to help librarians select books that will appeal to teens. It is named for Margaret Alexander ("Alex") Edwards, a young adult librarian who lived and worked in Baltimore. Edwards used adult books to help young adults understand the world around them. The books are selected by the Adult Books for Young Adults Task Force, a committee of the Young Adult Library Services Association.

Jane Gardam

Born: July 11, 1928; Coatham, Yorkshire, England

Jane Gardam is a writer equally at home with whatever fiction she writes, whether it is for children, young adults, or adults. She writes in a tradition of British children's and young adult fiction that is marked by social irony and domestic realism, as well as the characterization of gifted and independently-minded young people, often of unusual **middle-class** parents. Gardam's style is certainly sophisticated and literary. Her plots are often nostalgic of post-World War II Britain.

Gardam was born in a small town on England's Yorkshire coast, situated between moorland and unspoiled fishing villages and the huge industrial complexes of northeastern England. This region forms the setting for much of her fiction. After graduating from Bedford College, London in 1949, she took postgraduate classes until 1952, when she married lawyer David Gardam. She then worked in journalism in London until a family of two sons and a daughter arrived. She did not start writing fiction until her children were older, and published her first book, a series of short stories about an imaginative girl growing up, in 1971. The family had by then moved to Kent, on the coast of southern England.

Gardam's first young adult fiction, also published in 1971, was *A Long Way from Verona*. Her heroine, thirteen-year-old Jessica Vye, is the daughter of a brilliant teacher turned clergyman. She is

p.32

TITLES

A Long Way from Verona, 1971

The Summer After the Funeral, 1973

Bilgewater, 1976

The Hollow Land, 1981

Through the Doll's House Door, 1987

The Flight of the Maidens, 2000

brought up in his rather unconventional left-wing views, which are reinforced by her adventures into the back streets of the nearby industrial town, where she is nearly killed during a German air raid. The "Verona" of the book's title refers to the setting of William Shakespeare's late sixteenth century play *Romeo and Juliet*, which forms the subtext of Gardam's novel.

Gardam's next novel was *The Summer After the Funeral*, in which two sisters come to terms with the death of their clergyman father. Athene identifies closely with the English novelist Emily Brontë, herself the daughter of an austere Yorkshire clergyman. *Bilgewater* has a **boarding school** setting, as do p.16 several of Gardam's other novels. The heroine, Marigold Green, is the daughter of one of the teachers, and is herself, as Gardam was, a promising scholar, with good prospects for an academic career. However, she needs to come to terms with this.

The Hollow Land moves the setting to the p.26 **Westmorland** Fells, another wild area of northern England, where Gardam owned a second home. The stories reflect her love for the area p.32 and its culture, though she also explores **class** tensions. *Through the Doll's House Door* is, by contrast a **fantasy** story, which is unusual for p.87 Gardam. After a long gap, she returned to teenage heroines in *The Flight of the Maidens*, set in

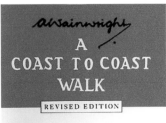
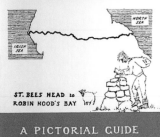

Westmorland

Westmorland is located in Cumbria. This area of England has many fells (barren highland areas). The area is well known as a place for walks. Alfred Wainwright (1907-1991) is known for his *Pictorial Guides to the Lakeland Fells*, seven books that he hand wrote and illustrated with his own drawings. These are regional walking guides and have become respected as regional works of art. In 1972, Wainwright described the Coast to Coast Walk in one of his books. It is a 190-mile footpath that crosses Northern England and is one of the most popular walks in the country.

YOUNG ADULT AUTHORS

Royal Society of Literature

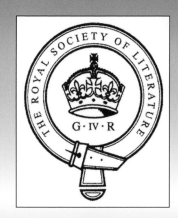

Founded in 1820 by Britain's King George IV, the Royal Society of Literature's (RSL) mission is to "reward literary merit and excite literary talent." It supports the needs and interests of writers and campaigns on their behalf in financial matters, such as the issue of taxation on books. It also attempts to purchase and preserve the literary archives of living writers, and maintains a cottage in Somerset, England for use by aspiring young writers and their families while work is in progress.

Ten times a year, lectures, discussions and readings are held for Fellows and members. The RSL also awards literary prizes and honors up to ten writers at one time as Companions of Literature for their outstanding achievements. Past winners include Winston Churchill.

the aftermath of World War II. It focuses on three sharply contrasting high school graduates waiting to go to college. It is essentially a coming-of-age novel, as the girls discover love, rebellion, escape, and left-wing politics. To some extent, Gardam is still writing the story of herself.

Jane Gardam has won the **Whitbread Award** twice, for *The Hollow Land* and for her adult fiction, *Queen of the Tambourine* (1991). Several other adult fictions have also won prizes. In 1985 she was made a **Fellow of the** Royal Society of Literature.

p.261

– David Barratt

Nancy Garden

Born: May 15, 1938; Boston, Massachusetts

www.members.aol.com/nancygarden

Although **Nancy Garden** has published almost thirty books, she is known primarily for her young adult novels dealing with homosexuality and homophobia. Because of the controversial nature of her subject matter, her works have stirred debate. Some of her books have even been banned from school and public libraries. However, she responded by making a similar act of censorship the subject of *The Year They Burned the Books*, which became a critically acclaimed novel. She has also worked to educate young people about threats to their First Amendment rights. The themes she addresses in all her work include bravery, faith in one's self and others, and personal integrity.

Private about her personal life, and even about her formative years, Garden has said that her parents read to her and told her stories when she was young. They also encouraged her to write, which she began doing at the age of eight. She initially aspired to become a veterinarian. During her young adulthood she did community theater work, was a professional actor for four seasons, and even did some Off-Broadway acting in New York City. However, after becoming discouraged by the difficulty of earning a living in the theater, she earned a master's degree in speech from Columbia Teacher's College and worked in the publishing industry. Her experience in pub-

p.57

p.74

lishing fueled her desire to see her own stories in print, and she soon began working toward that goal.

Garden's first books were published in 1971, but it was not until *Annie on My Mind* came out a decade later that she achieved widespread recognition. In that novel about homosexuality, two high school girls, one rich and the other poor, fall in love and secretly use the home of two lesbian teachers as a meeting place. When their relationship is discovered, the girls' families, their school, and their community erupt in anger. The revelation destroys the girls' relationship and costs the teachers whose home they have used, their jobs.

In *The Year They Burned the Books*, Jamie Crawford, the editor of her high school newspaper, stands up for her school's progressive sex-education curriculum against a new school board member who favors abstinence-only sex-education. Both sides become intractable, Jamie and some of her friends are gay-bashed, and "objectionable" books are burned before the novel's climax.

While Garden was among the first young adult authors to deal frankly with homosexuality and homophobia, her novels are not simply "problem" novels addressed to gay readers.

Homophobia

Homophobia is a fear, prejudice, or hatred toward homosexuals (males or females who are romantically or sexually interested in partners of the same sex), usually based upon irrational stereotypes. It can be expressed socially at many different levels, from a simple act such as school children teasing a gay classmate to more adult and horrific acts such as beatings or even the murder of presumed homosexuals. In Western society, this irrational hatred may stem from religious beliefs or fear of those who are different.

She strives to tell good stories about characters who seem real, believing that most teenagers can empathize with characters who are brutalized or made to feel subhuman, whatever the reasons.

p.45 Nancy Garden has received many writing honors. *Annie on My Mind* was named an American Library Association Best Book for Young Adults, p.480 and *The Year They Burned the Books* was a Lambda p.264 Book Award finalist. In 2001, Garden received the Robert B. Downs Intellectual Freedom Award for her efforts to defend her novel *Annie on My Mind* from being banned in a Kansas school district, as p.74 well as for her anticensorship work.

– Angela M. Salas

Lambda Literary Awards

The Lambda Literary Foundation is a national non-profit organization that recognizes and promotes gay and lesbian literature. Each year, a panel of judges selects 5 finalists in 20 categories from the hundreds of books submitted by publishers and other qualified professionals. The judges then select a single winning book in each category. The awards ceremony is held in a major city and is considered the literary award ceremony for gay and lesbian writers and the publishing community.

YOUNG ADULT AUTHORS

Leon Garfield

Born: July 14, 1921; Brighton, England
Died: June 2, 1996; London, England
www.ricochet-jeunes.org/eng/biblio/author/
garfield.html

Leon Garfield did not set out to write for young adults. He was persuaded to adapt his work for that audience because his stories seemed too p.198 **melodramatic** to be accepted by more mature readers. His readers may be grateful that he changed his target audience rather than toning down his work, because it allowed him to become the finest modern writer of an underrated art form. He followed up the swashbuckling sea adventure story *Jack Holborn* with *Devil-in-the-Fog*, in which a young member of a troupe of traveling players comes into a dangerous inheritance. He then published two fine accounts of life on the criminal fringes of eighteenth century English society, *Smith* and *Black Jack*. Garfield's melodramas often feature morally ambiguous characters—even the extraordinarily nasty villain of "The Simpleton" has a definite charisma—but he is always insistent on the necessity of an eventual redemption from evil.

Garfield's taste for melodrama was carried over .266 into the supernatural in the brilliant **Faustian** fantasies "Tom Corbett's Ghost" and *The Ghost Downstairs*. He produced two volumes of dramatizations of Greek mythology in collaboration with Edward Blishen. The **Carnegie Medal**-winning *The God* p.42 *Beneath the Sea* focuses on tales of the gods—using Hephaestus as a central character—while *The Golden Shadow* uses Heracles as the linchpin of a collection of hero-myths. Garfield also broadened his scope to embrace comedy in *The Strange Affair of Adelaide Harris*, a tale of misplaced children featur-

TITLES

Jack Holborn, 1964

Devil-in-the-Fog, 1966

Smith, 1967

Black Jack, 1968

Mr. Corbett's Ghost and Other Stories, 1968

The Drummer Boy, 1969

The Ghost Downstairs, 1970

The God Beneath the Sea, 1970 (with Edward Blishen)

The Strange Affair of Adelaide Harris, 1971

The Golden Shadow, 1973 (with Edward Blishen)

The Sound of Coaches, 1974

The Prisoners of September, 1975

The Cloak, 1976

The Lamplighter's Funeral, 1976

Mirror, Mirror, 1976

Moss and Blister, 1976

The Pleasure Garden, 1976

The Dumb Cake, 1977

The Fool, 1977

Labour in Vain, 1977

ing the magnificently inept detective Selwyn Raven, and its sequel, *Bostock and Harris*.

When Garfield moderated his melodramatic tendencies it was not to adapt his work to an older audience but to bring into sharp focus the working lives of pre-Victorian children. His contributions to an established series of educational works for younger readers, begun with *The Boy and His Monkey* (1969), formed an overture to his own magisterial fifteen-part series *The Apprentices*. Some of his later works, including *The December Rose* and *The Empty Sleeve*, also feature **apprentices** who become involved with exotic mysteries. Others, including *The Confidence Man* and *The Sound of Coaches*, are sophisticated picaresque tales. In the **Whitbread Award**-winning *John Diamond*, William Jones, on discovering that his late father was a swindler, sets off for London to right the wrongs done to the unfortunate title character. Broader concerns are also evident in *The Prisoners of September*, which features two friends separated by their opposite attitudes to the French Revolution, and *The Wedding Ghost*, a beautiful allegory. *The Blewcoat Boy* revisits the criminal underworld of *Smith*, but in a much lighter vein.

Leon Garfield has often been called a "Dicken-

p.24

Faustian

Faustian refers to the character of Dr. Faustus. The tale of Faustus, told in many versions, is that of a man of great learning who enters into a pact with the Devil. In the tale's earliest forms, the story teaches that turning away from God may lead to temporary pleasures but ultimately leads to disaster. Today, the adjective "Faustian" refers to someone who sacrifices the spiritual life for knowledge or possessions in the material world.

The Mystery of Edwin Drood

British novelist Charles Dickens was writing *The Mystery of Edwin Drood* when he died suddenly in 1870. His final novel was left half finished. Almost immediately, other writers began offering their versions of the story Dickens intended. In fact, a play of the unfinished book even allows the audience to choose Drood's murderer. It is undoubtedly the most popular unfinished mystery story in literary history.

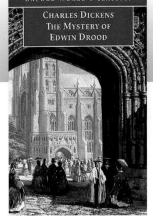

sian" writer (he is one of several writers to have attempted a conclusion to Charles Dickens's *The Mystery of Edwin Drood*); however, the subject matter of his young adult fiction is more closely akin to the work of Henry Fielding or novels by Dickens's sensationalist contemporaries Edward Bulwer-Lytton and W. Harrison Ainsworth set in the eighteenth century. Garfield is, however, a more accomplished stylist than Ainsworth or Lytton, and his moral sensibility is that of a literary artist.

– Brian Stableford

Alan Garner

Born: October 17, 1934; Congleton, Cheshire, England

www.fantasticfiction.co.uk/authors/Alan_Garner

Alan Garner grew up in the west-central English county of Cheshire, an area that has a strongly Celtic influence in its local folklore. Alderley Edge, a place located near where he grew up, is the site where a mummified first century druid, Lindow Man, was discovered in 1983. The same site is the locale of many of Garner's stories. After attending Manchester Grammar School, Garner studied classics at Magdalen College, Oxford, but left without taking a degree. He has worked as a documentary writer and director for British television, but through most of his life, he has been simply a writer.

p.269

Garner's first novel, *The Weirdstone of Brisingamen*, is the story of two children, Susan and Colin, who are sent to Alderley for six months and find themselves involved in a battle to save the world. They encounter evil and good elves, dwarves, and a wizard. The story is based on the widespread legend of King **Arthur's** sleeping knights, who are expected to wake to save England in its darkest hour; the weirdstone, which is necessary for their waking, turns out to be Susan's (stolen) bracelet. In Garner's sequel, *The Moon of Gomrath*, Susan and Colin inadvertently waken the Wild Hunt (another widespread legend) and must battle to restrain the forces of evil.

p.4

Elidor is another story set near Manchester. In this novel, the four Wat-

Lindow Man

In 1984, while cutting peat (a decaying form of plants used as fuel) in Lindow Moss, Andy Mould discovered the mummified remains of a man. Police removed the block of peat containing the mummy from the bog and turned it over to scientists to discover who this man was and if he had been recently murdered. Five days later they identified the mummy as a man who had been murdered almost two thousand years ago. Scientists determined that Lindow Man had died between A.D. 50 and A.D. 100, and that he may have been the victim of a ritual sacrifice. The mummy can now be found in the British Museum in London, England.

son children stumble across the magical realm of Elidor and become the guardians of its treasures: a sword, spear, stone, and cauldron (based on the four treasures of the Túatha Dé Danann of Irish mythology). The children must safeguard the treasures and seal the boundaries between the mortal and magical realms to prevent them from being captured by the forces of evil.

The Owl Service is based on the medieval Welsh tale of the tragic marriage of the god Lleu Llaw Gyffes and his wife Blodeuwedd, the woman made of flowers who is turned into an owl as the price for her betrayal of him. This story begins to repeat itself in the modern age when Alison and her stepbrother Roger discover a set of plates with an abstract flower design, which when traced turns into the picture of an owl and disappears. Garner does not merely retell the story as a modern fairy tale, however; he uses the story as a means of incorporating modern questions of class, sexuality, and English/Celtic nationalism into his narrative.

Redshift is acknowledged as a difficult novel, in which three versions of the same narrative take

Aborigines

The native people of a land are called aborigines. When capitalized, the term also identifies the native people of Australia. Australian Aborigines are believed to have lived there for more than fifty thousand years before Captain Cook discovered the island continent in 1788. They suffered a

similar fate to the Native Americans when their homeland was colonized: illness, displacement, slavery, violence, and discrimination. In recent times Aborigines have lobbied for their rights. In 1967, their claims to land were recognized and they now hold 9.6 percent of all land in Australia.

place at three different periods (Roman Britain and the seventeenth and twentieth centuries). *Standloper*, likewise, is a complex tale of an eighteenth century Cheshire man who is convicted of holding a "pagan" ritual and is sent to Australia, where he ultimately is adopted by Aborigines as the incarnation of their god Murrnagurk. Both novels are linguistically complex, as Garner does his best to recreate the speech and thought patterns of his characters in a historically accurate way.

p.461 p.27

Alan Garner has also published a number of books of children's stories, most of them also based on Welsh and Celtic mythology, although more directly told than his young adult works. His writing honors include Britain's Carnegie Medal for *The Owl Service* and a 1996 Phoenix Award for *The Stone Book*, which he had published twenty years earlier.

p.147 p.42

— Leslie Ellen Jones

Jean Craighead George

Born: July 2, 1919; Washington, D.C.

www.jeancraigheadgeorge.com

Jean Craighead George's novels for young adults portray lively and talented young people who must learn to combine the familiar old ways of their heritage with the demands of the future. Their families are often disrupted by environmental and social change, and the youths learn self-reliance from animal as well as human rivals and friends. By connecting to nature, her characters realize the value of wilderness and the need for balance between development and preservation.

As George grew up, she closely observed the many animals with which she came into contact, especially during family camping trips. She was taught the value of exploration by her naturalist parents and often fantasized about embarking upon a survival adventure of her own. Following up on these interests, she majored in both science and literature in college. Afterward, she worked as a reporter and member of the **White House press corps**, but after becoming a young mother, she again focused on her love of nature. At home she began encouraging animal visitors, including such diverse species as minks and tarantulas.

George's first novel, *My Side of the Mountain* (1959), dramatizes her childhood ambition of living alone in the woods and displays her knowledge of falconry. In this book for younger readers, her young **protagonist** survives for a year on his own in the Catskill Mountains with only a falcon for a companion.

In 1973 George wrote her first novel for young

.272

p.233

TITLES

adults—*Julie of the Wolves*, which was inspired by her discovery that wolves are friendly, social animals, communicating through sounds, movements, and scents. To understand these complex creatures, she visited a naval research laboratory in Barrow, Alaska, where she learned to interact with wolves. As in all George's works, this novel is carefully researched and draws on her personal experiences with animals, nature, and outdoor activity. Many of George's readers loved the title character of *Julie of the Wolves* so much that they persuaded her to write a sequel. Eventually, she wrote three books about this Inupiat **Eskimo** girl and the **wolf pack** that saves her life on the Alaskan tundra. Another of her books, *Water Sky*, features a young man from New England who visits the same region. George has also placed stories in the Mexican fishing culture on the Island of Coronado and in the Seminole Indian culture in Florida.

p.534

p.273

Jean George's spirited adventures in which young people learn to face adult challenges are timeless.

White House Press Corps

The White House press corps is the group of journalists who report on the president's actions and on other activities in the White House. They are given press passes that allow them to meet in a room in the White House for a daily briefing by the president's press secretary. The reporters from newspapers, magazines, and television scramble to ask questions and get answers that they can use in their news stories. They also receive press releases, which are printed statements from the White House. Occasionally, the president will hold a press conference and verbally answer questions posed by press corp members. Reporters from the group travel along with the president on matters of national interest.

Wolf Packs

Wolves are one of the best-known examples of animals that form packs to hunt together and to rear offspring. Most packs are made up of fewer than eight members. Two packs may come together temporarily. One pack may accept some members of the other pack and chase unwanted members away. A pack can produce up to six cubs a year. The members of the pack hunt for food together. Once they have consumed a kill, they will go out to hunt again. Wolves hunt frequently; they look for young, old, and sick prey. Pack behavior seems to be based on cooperation between related wolves.

Her characters draw on their personal resources and on the living world around them. Her novel *My Side of the Mountain* was a **Newbery Honor Book** in 1960 and was made into a movie in 1969. She also won the **Newbery Medal** for *Julie of the Wolves* in 1973 and has since received many additional awards. In recent years George has worked with an artist to illustrate her books and with a composer to add the sounds of nature to her recorded works.

– Margaret A. Dodson

p.102

Barbara Snow Gilbert

Born: April 9, 1954; Oklahoma City, Oklahoma

www.teenreads.com/authors/au-gilbert-barbara.asp

Barbara Snow Gilbert's books take on diverse themes, but through them runs a common thread: young people faced with difficult choices. Her maturing characters must search inside themselves to examine their convictions and to find the courage to act on them.

An attorney by training, Gilbert capitalized on her experience with legal issues in her first published novel *Stone Water*. When the grandfather of young protagonist, Grant Hues, is transferred to a hospital's ward for terminal cases, Grant must decide whether to respect the dying man's wish to avoid life support. Through Grant's exchanges with his lawyer father, the legal and ethical issues surrounding assisted suicide unfold. Gilbert has said that the challenges her young characters face would be difficult for people of any age. As a result, her characters grow strong.

In *Broken Chords*, seventeen-year-old Clara spends hours practicing the repetitive arpeggios or "broken chords" that give the book its title. However, the book's title also has another meaning, relating to Clara's striving to achieve harmony in her life. A gifted pianist, Clara is poised to capture a coveted prize that will assure her a place at the Juilliard School of Music. However, although she is technically proficient, she begins to doubt whether a career in music will make her happy. On the other hand, she worries that without her music she has no identity. In the metaphor of the Russian folktale that pervades the story, she feels herself melting

p.233

p.1

p.275

like a snow-person who is lovingly, but imprudently, taken indoors to be sheltered by a fireplace.

Gilbert has said that her legal work does not directly influence her writing, but that controversial issues interest her. In her third novel, *Paper Trail*, she set out to write a story about fear coming from a source that is contemporary, real, and much on the public mind. Spurred by the devastating bombing of a federal building in Oklahoma City (where she was born) in 1995, she did extensive research on right-wing militia and paramilitary organizations. Her story of Walker, an Oklahoma teenager who has lived his life amongst the "Soldiers of God," begins when he sees his mother murdered. He flees into the woods to evade pursuers after learning that his father is an undercover FBI agent whose mission is infiltration. Walker's struggle to survive, along with uncertainty over his father's fate—both of which turn out to be hallucinations—are intermingled with excerpts from media and government reports quoting real-life militia members. Their hatred and violence provide a stark background against which Walker's attempts to understand his past, present, and future play out.

Juilliard School

In 1905, Dr. Frank Damrosch, the head of music education for New York City's public schools, founded the Institute of Musical Art. He wanted American music students to have a place where they could receive first-class musical training without traveling abroad. When August Juilliard died in 1919, he left money to found the Juilliard Graduate School, another school designed to train musicians. It was opened in 1924, and it merged with the Institute in 1926 to become the Juilliard School of Music. With the addition of a Dance Division in 1951 and a Drama Division in 1968, the name became simply the Juilliard School. Juilliard has been located at Lincoln Center, New York City's performing arts center, since 1969.

Barbara Gilbert's teenage characters are strong and honest. Her themes are challenging. For these reasons, *School Library Journal* named *Stone Water* a **Best Book of the Year** in 1996. The **New York Public Library** included it in their 1997 list of **Best Books for Teens**. Gilbert also received **Oklahoma Book Awards** for both *Stone Water* and *Broken Chords*.

p.195

p.276

p.15

– Faith Hickman Brynie

Oklahoma Book Award

The Oklahoma Book Award is given each year to an Oklahoma author who has written about Oklahoma. Awards are given for fiction, non-fiction, children or young adult fiction, poetry, and design or illustration. The program is sponsored by the Oklahoma Center for the Book, an affiliate of the Center for the Book in the Library of Congress. In 1968, Oklahoma became the fourth state to establish a Center for the Book.

Mel Glenn

Born: May 10, 1943; Zurich, Switzerland

www.melglenn.com

Mel Glenn has written poetry and several novels but is best known for what might be termed the novel in poems: books in which poems by multiple narrators and from different points of view are arranged to tell a story. Glenn retired from teaching high school in 2001 but continues as a mentor to new teachers in New York City. He primarily writes on topics relevant to teenage life such as school, sports, love, friendship, family, and violence. However, he has also written more conventional novels for a younger audience.

Glenn was born in Switzerland, but his family moved to Brooklyn, New York, when he was just three years old. After graduating from New York University with a degree in English, he spent two years in Sierra Leone with the **Peace Corps**. He returned to New York, earned his master's degree from **Yeshiva University**, and began teaching at his own alma mater, Abraham Lincoln High School. In 1980, on a dare from his wife, he began writing his first book of poems, *Class Dismissed! High School Poems*, which was well received and marked the beginning of a successful career inspired largely by his students.

Jump Ball: A Basketball Season in Poems concerns a tragic bus accident that kills and injures several members of Tower High School's basketball team on their way to the state championship. The narrative develops through a series of **stream-of-consciousness** poems, interspersed with news broadcasts, school public address announcements,

p.224
p.278
p.279

TITLES

Yeshiva University

Yeshiva University is a state chartered university founded in 1927 in New York City. It is a Jewish university and offers excellent programs in liberal arts, science, business and Jewish studies. It is among the top fifty research universities in the country. YU has professional programs in medicine, law, social work, psychology, Jewish studies, and Jewish education. It has a unique undergraduate program that allows students to have a dual major in both Jewish studies and another discipline.

and conversations, and ends with a list of the dead and injured. *Who Killed Mr. Chippendale? A Mystery in Poems* uses the same technique to investigate the murder of a high school English teacher, shot to death while taking his morning jog. His life and the manner of his death are examined through the various perspectives of students and staff. Glenn employed this method again in *The Taking of Room 114: A Hostage Drama in Poems* to describe a high school teacher who takes his senior history class hostage at gunpoint. The situation is explored through poems by the teacher, his students, and other characters.

Glenn's more conventional novels for school-age children include *Play-by-Play*, in which the usually uncoordinated Jeremy discovers an unexpected talent for soccer, which causes problems with his overly competitive friend Lloyd. The relationship between Lloyd and Jeremy, whose sense of fair play is as strong as his soccer skills, forms the central conflict in this book. The same characters reappear in *Squeeze Play*, in which the featured sport is baseball, at which Jeremy is not very good; this time his conflict is with his disciplinarian teacher.

Mel Glenn's writing honors include a nomination for the prestigious **Edgar Allan Poe Award** of the Mystery Writers of America. He has received the **Christopher Award** and the American Library Association has recognized many of his books as **Best Books for Young Adults**, and named *Who Killed Mr. Chippendale?* as one of the **Top Ten Books of the Year**. *Class Dismissed! High School Poems* won the Society of Children's Book Writers and Illustrators Golden Kite Award.

p.72

p.45

.480

p.11

p.111

– Mary Virginia Davis

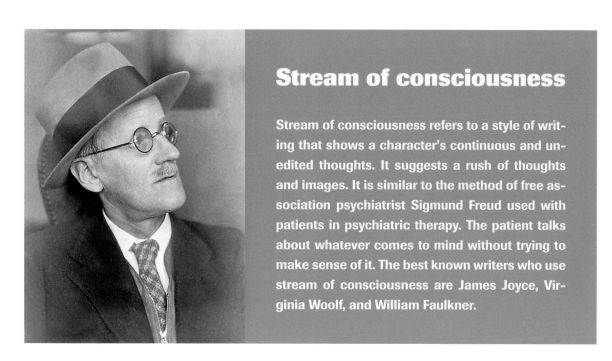

Stream of consciousness

Stream of consciousness refers to a style of writing that shows a character's continuous and unedited thoughts. It suggests a rush of thoughts and images. It is similar to the method of free association psychiatrist Sigmund Freud used with patients in psychiatric therapy. The patient talks about whatever comes to mind without trying to make sense of it. The best known writers who use stream of consciousness are James Joyce, Virginia Woolf, and William Faulkner.

William Golding

Born: September 19, 1911; Newquay, Cornwall, England
Died: June 19, 1993; Perranarworthal, Cornwall, England

www.william-golding.co.uk

TITLES

Lord of the Flies, 1954

The Inheritors, 1955

Novelist **William Golding** typically placed his characters in physically challenging or isolated situations. The difficult choices his characters must make to survive are also moral choices that shape the courses of their lives. Golding's ability to examine important issues through exciting and readable stories made him a **best-selling** writer and brought him many important literary awards, including the highest distinction of all, the Nobel Prize in Literature. p.384 p.23

Golding was born and grew up in the southwestern region of England known as Cornwall. As a child he read constantly, ranging from the plays of William Shakespeare to the popular adventure stories of American novelist Edgar Rice Burroughs (author of the Tarzan book series). As a young man, Golding attended Oxford University and eventually followed in his father's footsteps by becoming a schoolmaster, although he rejected his father's field of science in favor of literature. World War II interrupted Golding's career and taught him a lesson about the human capacity for evil. It was a lesson that he would dramatize years later in his first published novel, *Lord of the Flies*. p.17

The Coral Island

The Coral Island was written by R. M. Ballantyne and first published in 1858. It tells the story of three English boys, Ralph, Jack, and Peterkin, who are shipwrecked on a deserted island in the Pacific Ocean. They must build a shelter, make fire, gather fruit and other food, and build boats to explore the neighboring islands. Unlike the boys in *Lord of the Flies*, they get along and behave well. They are finally rescued by an English missionary and return to England with two friendly natives. They have become more experienced and much wiser from their time on the island.

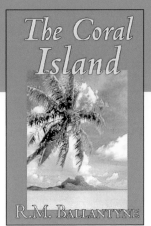

Lord of the Flies relates the experiences of a group of British schoolboys who are being evacuated from England during a war in the near future. When their plane crashes on a small uninhabited island, they are the only survivors. Rather than cooperating with one another for their mutual survival, most of the boys descend into savagery and warfare—just as their elders have done. The book recalls an adventure novel with a happier outcome that had been popular with young readers for more than one hundred years, R. M. Ballantyne's *The Coral Island* (1858). After serving in Britain's Royal Navy during World War II, Golding was unable to share Ballantyne's rosy view of human nature. He wrote *Lord of the Flies* to counter what he thought was Ballantyne's unrealistic optimism about the human character.

p.281

Although *Lord of the Flies* received good reviews on its release in 1954, it did not achieve great popularity until the 1960's, when young people started seriously questioning adult authority and found the book's themes appealing. It has been assigned in schools and read widely ever since and has also been filmed twice.

Golding also wrote his second novel, *The Inheritors*, as a response to an earlier work—*Outline of History* (1920) by novelist and social critic H. G. Wells. Golding's book is written from the point of

James Tait Black Memorial Prizes

Founded in memory of a partner in the publishing house of A. & C. Black Ltd., the James Tait Black Memorial Prizes have been awarded since 1919 and are among the oldest and most respected in Great Britain. Every year two prizes of £3,000 are awarded for the best book of fiction and the best biography published in the past twelve months. Publishers submit books for consideration. The author can be from any country, but the submitted books must be written in English and first published in the United Kingdom. An author can win the prize only once for both fiction and biography.

view of a prehistorical Neanderthal man named Lok. Whereas Wells had characterized Neanderthals as primitive and brutish, Golding depicted them as noble if limited, lacking the cunning and violent nature of modern humanity's direct ancestors, the Cro-Magnons.

Most of Golding's later works were critically praised but proved less popular with readers. *Darkness Visible* (1979) is the story of a young man horribly burned in the German bombing of England in World War II. Golding's trilogy *Rites of Passage* (1980), *Close Quarters* (1987), and *Fire Down Below* (1989) describes a voyage from Britain to Australia p.461 in the early nineteenth century.

For his whole body of work, William Golding received the **Nobel Prize in Literature** in 1983. *Darkness Visible* was awarded one of Britain's most important literary prizes, the James Tait Black p.282 Memorial Prize, and *Rites of Passage* won Britain's other main literary award, the **Booker McConnell Prize**.

– Margaret A. Dodson

Elizabeth Goudge

Born: April 24, 1900; Wells, Somerset, England
Died: April 1, 1984; near Henley-on-Thames, England

The **best-selling** novels of **Elizabeth Goudge** have appealed primarily to adult women and adolescent girls. Many of her stories of family life were inspired by the places in which she lived and by people whom she knew during her tranquil childhood. Although she never married, she also wrote compelling novels about romantic love.

Elizabeth de Beauchamp Goudge (pronounced "goozsh") was born in Wells, Somerset, England, the only child of an Anglican clergyman and his wife, a talented storyteller. Many of Goudge's novels are set in cathedral towns such as Wells and Ely, where she spent her own childhood; others were inspired by her holiday visits to her grandparents on the **Channel Island** of Guernsey.

Though as a child Goudge wrote fairy tales and poetry, she did not try making writing her profession until she was nineteen and a student at the Reading University School of Art. The first book of stories that she published at that time did not sell well, and none of her plays had more than a single performance. It was her first novel, *Island Magic*, that launched Goudge's literary career when she was thirty-four. This suspenseful story of a Guernsey farm couple, their five children, and the mysterious stranger who comes to

384

284

their rescue in an emergency was admired both in Great Britain and in the United States.

A vacation trip to Scotland gave Goudge the idea for her first love story, *The Middle Window*. When this story's heroine, a young English woman named Judith Cameron, visits Scotland, she keeps feeling that she has been there before. The places she sees and the people whom she meets, even a young Scottish laird (lord), all are somehow familiar. After dreaming about another Judith, who lost her husband in the Jacobite uprising of 1745, she makes a momentous decision. She breaks off with her English fiancé and stays in Scotland with the laird.

Romance is also important in Goudge's historical novels. p.11 Two separate love stories figure in *Towers in the Mist*, and *The Child from the Sea* recounts the story of Lucy Walter's disastrous involvement with England's seventeenth century king Charles II.

Goudge's most famous novel was based on her great-uncle's true story. In *Green Dolphin Street*, two sisters are both in love with a man who lives in New Zealand. p.456 When he writes to their father in England

Channel Islands

This small group of islands in the English Channel is located eighty miles south of England but only fourteen miles off the French coast. The islands have belonged to the English Crown since 1066. Their total area is seventy-five square miles. Only two of the islands, Guernsey and Jersey, are inhabited. They have a combined population of about 150,000 people. The main sources of income in the islands are tourists, finance, and raising livestock, particularly dairy cows.

Ireland

United Kingdom

English Channel

Guernsey →

Jersey →

Atlantic Ocean

France

M-G-M Literary Award

In 1947, the Metro-Goldwyn-Mayer (M-G-M) movie studios created a literary award as a way to get the rights to make a film out of a popular book. In total, M-G-M bought five books this way, *Green Dolphin Street*, being one of them. Of the five, only *Green Dolphin Street* and *Raintree County* (1957) became films. The film version of Goudge's novel was released in 1947 and won Academy Awards for visual effects and sound effects. The studio had spent a lot of money filming the story and was disappointed to not win more awards.

to request the hand of one of the sisters in marriage, he accidentally writes the name of the sister whom he does not love. When the wrong sister arrives in New Zealand, he feels honor-bound to marry her, and his true love becomes a nun. When the man and his wife return to England forty years later, the sisters learn the truth and become reconciled. *Green Dolphin Street* sold a million copies, still remains in print, and won Goudge an **M-G-M Literary Award** of $125,000. The film version of the novel was a box office hit. p.285

Elizabeth Goudge owed her initial popularity mostly to her imaginative plots and her strong women characters. However, her books have remained popular because they express so sincerely her love of life and her faith in the power of goodness.

— Rosemary M. Canfield Reisman

Steven Gould

Born: February 7, 1955; Fort Huachuca, Arizona

Steven Gould's work does not fit neatly into young adult genres. While it is true that his protagonists are frequently adolescent boys who are coming of age, his subject matter is typically sophisticated, and his writing is complex. He strives to write for two audiences; he wants to speak to young adults without talking down to them, while holding the interest of his adult readers. Most of the time, he achieves this difficult goal.

p.233

While growing up in such exotic places as Taiwan and Thailand, Gould was drawn to reading science fiction, which helped him escape from an unhappy family situation. After finishing college, he worked as a database programmer and focused on his own writing. In 1980 he published his first story, "The Touch of Their Eyes," in the science-fiction magazine *Analog*. Afterward, he published one story a year for ten years in *Analog*, *Amazing*, and *Asimov's Science Fiction Magazine*. One of his stories was nominated for a Nebula Award, two others for **Hugo Awards**.

p.287

Gould's first two novels, featuring eighteen-year-old male protagonists, are his books that are most geared to young adult audiences. In *Jumper*, Davy Rice, the narrator, escapes horrible situations, such as a beating from his alcoholic father, through teleportation. In *Wildside*, Charlie Newell finds a world filled with extinct animals and then shares his find with his friends. In both novels Gould creates sensitive and likeable protagonists with whom older teens can identify.

p.10

Gould's third novel is a departure for him. Co-written with his wife, Laura Mixon, a science-fiction writer herself, *Greenwar* is the fast-moving story about a terrorist group trying to destroy a hydrogen farm and marine-research station. The story is told from three points of view—those of Emma Tooke, an engineer; Gabriel, the leader of the terrorists; and Keith, an Environmental Protection Agency agent. Set in a plausible future world, *Greenwar* focuses on adventure and politics.

Helm also features an adolescent who is coming of age, but it is set in another world after Earth has been destroyed. Its plot revolves around Leland de Laal, who disobeys his father when he puts on the powerful glass helm, the colony's connection with knowledge about Earth. *Blind Waves* is also set in the future when Earth's polar ice caps have melted, causing the oceans to rise (the Deluge) and people to lose their homes. In this book, the female protagonist, Salvage operator Patricia Beenan, stumbles on a sunken barge filled with the dead bodies of illegal immigrants. She soon becomes involved in a dangerous web of politics and corruption, played out against the Texas Gulf Coast setting. In all these novels, Gould draws on his knowledge of scuba diving, martial arts and the oil industry.

Nebula Award

The Science Fiction Writers of American grant the Nebula Award each year to honor excellence in science fiction and fantasy writing. Awards are given for best short story, novelette, novella, novel, and script. A work is eligible for twelve months after its first publication, production, or first release in the U.S. Only active members of the association may recommend and vote for Nebula Awards.

Compton Crook Award

The Baltimore Science Fiction Society awards the Compton Crook Award for best first novel in science fiction, fantasy, or horror at Balticon, its annual convention held each year on Memorial Day. Crook was a professor of natural history at Towson State University and wrote under the name of Stephen Tall. He died in 1981, and the first award was granted in 1982 for the best first novel of 1982. The winning author receives a check for $750 and is treated as Guest of Honor at Balticon.

Besides telling a good story, Steven Gould's books question environmental and social issues without being didactic. He received numerous awards for *Jumper* including the **Compton Crook Award Final Ballot**, the **American Library Association's Best Books for Young Adults** award, and a citation on the International Teachers' Association's **Recommended Reading List**.

– Cassandra Kircher

 p.45

 p.288

 p.480

John Grisham

Born: February 8, 1955; Jonesboro, Arkansas

www.randomhouse.com/features/grisham

Most of **John Grisham**'s novels are set within the world of law. Southern courtrooms and law offices are the most common backdrops for his legal thrillers. Each story's main character is usually a lawyer who needs to use his intelligence and logic to outsmart other lawyers, criminals, prosecutors, and judges. A common theme in his novels is a young, poor and inexperienced lawyer who uses his brains to outsmart people richer and more powerful than himself. The twist and turns of the plot create action and suspense.

Grisham was born and reared in Arkansas. The son of a cotton farmer, he dreamed of playing professional baseball as a boy. He ended up going into law, however, and graduated from Mississippi State University law school in 1981. He worked as a criminal defense and personal injury lawyer for almost ten years before retiring to devote time to his writing. He also served six years as a representative to the Mississippi State House of Representatives.

Grisham's first book, *A Time to Kill*, was inspired by a real-life criminal case and explores what happens when the victims of a crime take the law into their own hands. Grisham wrote the book while still practicing law; six days a week he would arrive at his office at 5:00 A.M. to get his writing in before the work day began. The book took him three years to finish and was rejected by many publishers before finally seeing print in 1989.

Grisham's next book, *The Firm*, about a young lawyer starting work at what appears to be the per-

TITLES

A Time to Kill, 1989

The Firm, 1991

The Pelican Brief, 1992

The Client, 1993

The Chamber, 1994

The Rainmaker, 1995

The Runaway Jury, 1996

The Partner, 1997

The Testament, 1999

The Brethren, 2000

A Painted House, 2001

Skipping Christmas, 2001

The Summons, 2002

Bleachers, 2003

The King of Torts, 2003

The Last Juror, 2004

fect law firm, became the **best-selling** novel of 1991 and was made into a successful movie. Throughout the 1990's Grisham wrote one novel a year, and all of them became best-sellers, making him one of the best-selling novelists of that decade. Most of these books have been made into **popular movies**.

p.384

p.29

In 2001 Grisham departed from writing about law with two novels: *A Painted House* and *Skipping Christmas. A Painted House* is based on his childhood in rural Arkansas. It explores one summer in the life of a young farm boy growing up amid cotton fields in the 1950's. Luke, the novel's seven-year-old narrator, loves baseball but must help his family harvest cotton from the eighty acres they rent. As he picks cotton and plays ball and listens to the adults around him, Luke learns a terrible secret that will change his life forever.

p.291

Skipping Christmas is a humorous and satirical look at what happens when a husband and wife decide to ignore the Christmas holiday and all of the chaos and craziness that surrounds it by taking a cruise. A 2004 movie, *Christmas with the Kranks*, was based on this novel.

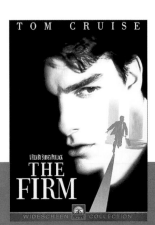

Novel into Film

While John Grisham enjoys a reputation as a best-selling author, his books are also adapted into movies that also are box-office successes. In the ten year period between 1993 and 2003, eight of his novels were made into films. Together they made nearly $800,000,000 at box offices worldwide. The movie rights to *A Time to Kill* alone brought Grisham $6,000,000 and final script and cast approval.

Cotton

Cotton is an important crop. It is grown in fourteen of the United States. It is a fiber, feed, and food crop. As a fiber, cotton is spun at textile mills. It then is woven into fabric for clothing, sheets, tow-els, and many other products we use daily. The seed is crushed to produce oil, meal, and hulls. The oil is used in cooking and salad dressings. The meal and hull is used in feed for livestock, chicken, and fish and as fertilizer.

John Grisham remains interested in baseball. He has built six baseball fields on his property for use by Little League teams and serves as the local Little League commissioner. He also does work for charitable groups and his church group. John Grisham lives with his family in Oxford, Mississippi.

– Deborah DePiero

Judith Guest

Born: March 29, 1936; Detroit, Michigan

Judith Guest writes books for adult readers, but some of them have young adults as their central characters, and mature young adults read her books with great pleasure. Guest's novel, *Ordinary People*, is especially popular with young adult readers. Guest graduated from the University of Michigan with a bachelor's degree in education and taught in public schools in Michigan. The experience gave her insights into the personalities of young adults. She is a meticulous craftsperson who works very carefully and slowly on her books.

Ordinary People is the story of Conrad Jarrett, who is eighteen when the book begins, and his family. After his brother Buck drowns while the two are sailing, Conrad tries to commit suicide. With the help of his father, friends, and especially Tyrone Berger, his psychiatrist, Conrad makes the hard trip out of depression as he comes to grips with his problems, especially those involving his relationship with his mother, Beth, and with his feelings about himself. He gradually learns to like himself and to see his staying alive as a good thing. The story also focuses on Conrad's father, Calvin, as he reassesses his role as a father and husband.

Second Heaven also treats a troubled young man, Gale Murray, who is abused by his father. When Gale's father tries to have him institutionalized, a friend named Catherine Holzmann tries to prevent the father from having his way, with the help of a lawyer, Michael Atwood. Catherine and Michael both have problems of their own, especially those involving the growing relationship between them. Nevertheless they work hard to save Gale, even though Michael feels that Gale is hostile toward him and arrogant.

Errands again treats family problems. Early in the book, the father, Keith Browner, dies of cancer. Before his death, the members of the family are all close. His death causes economic and emotional problems for his wife, Annie, and their three children, especially his older son, thirteen-year-old Harry. Annie becomes involved with finding work and then becoming comfortable in her job. As a result, she pays less attention to her children than she did when her husband was alive. Harry begins to roam the streets and hang out with a rough group of teenagers. When a fishing hook that Harry is using almost blinds his younger brother, Jimmy, Harry begins to work his way through his serious emotional problems, and the family starts to come together again as a functioning unit.

Guest's novels tend to involve powerful emotions and complex interactions among characters. Several of her books involve experiments in

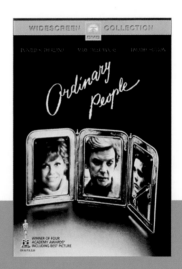

Ordinary People, the Movie

The 1980 film version of *Ordinary People* is a faithful adaptation of Guest's novel. The first major movie directed by actor Robert Redford, it won both audience attention and awards. A serious movie in a period of light comedy films, it received Academy Awards for Best Picture, Best Director, Best Screenplay, and Best Supporting Actor. It is interesting for people who have read the book to also see the film and compare their impressions of both.

using third-person limited point of view, a technique that Guest uses especially well in *Ordinary People*. Her novels treat sympathetically some of the most serious emotional problems that young adults face. Although her works are challenging to read, they speak directly to young adults.

p.294

The Susan B. Anthony Institute for Gender and Women's Studies and the Department of English at the University of Rochester awarded Judith Guest the **Janet Heidinger Kafka Prize** for fiction by an American woman in 1976 for *Ordinary People*. In 1980, the novel was made into a motion picture that won several Academy Awards, including best picture.

p.29

– Richard Tuerk

Janet Heidinger Kafka Prize

The Kafka Prize was first given in 1976 by the Susan B. Anthony Institute for Gender and Women's Studies and the Department of English at the University of Rochester in New York. It is awarded each year to a U.S. woman writer for a work of fiction. The prize is named for a young editor who was killed in an automobile accident at age thirty. Her family, friends, and colleagues in publishing raised the money that provides for the prize. Each year, publishers nominate candidates whom they think have written the best novels, short story collections, or experimental works.

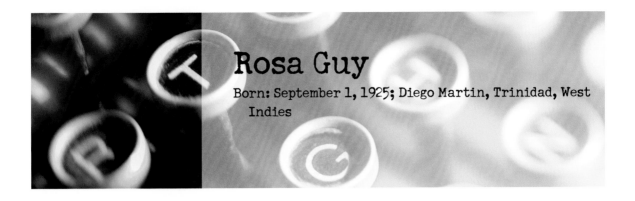

Rosa Guy

Born: September 1, 1925; Diego Martin, Trinidad, West Indies

Rosa Guy has earned wide acclaim for her young adult fiction. Her books for young readers address the poverty, prejudice, and violence that so often characterize the lives of people living in large urban areas. Her young adult fiction also addresses specific social and racial challenges facing immigrants of African descent in the United States.

Born in the **West Indies** country of Trinidad, Guy and her younger sister, Ameze, emigrated to the United States in 1932 to join their parents in New York City's **Harlem**. After the death of her mother in 1934 and her father three years later, Guy lived in a succession of **foster homes** for several years. She dropped out of high school and found work in a garment factory to support herself and her sister. There she met Warner Guy, whom she married in 1941 and with whom she had a son, Warner Guy, Jr.

While her husband served overseas in the military during World War II, Guy took an interest in writing and theater. She attended classes at New York University and studied acting at the American Negro Theater. She moved to Connecticut with her husband following his return from the war. After they divorced in 1950, Guy returned to New York and her job at the factory.

In 1951 Guy helped found the **Harlem Writers Guild**, a writing workshop that later included such celebrated black authors as Maya Angelou and Walter Mosley. Initially interested in writing drama,

Harlem

Harlem is a part of New York City and home to the largest African American community in the U.S. A small group of blacks first moved there in the early twentieth century. By 1920, more than two hundred and fifty thousand blacks lived there. Harlem represented both the best and the worst of city life. In the 1920's, it was home to a cultural awakening called the Harlem Renaissance; writers, musicians, entertainers, and artists enjoyed the creative environment. But there was also poverty and crime that crowded city living encourages. Many areas of Harlem had declined by the 1970's. The city began to take measures to improve neighborhood life. Today, the area and old housing is undergoing a period of revival and renewal . Movement of new citizens into Harlem has encouraged the return of shops, restaurants, and other services as well.

Guy soon turned to fiction. She published two short stories in 1960, and her first novel, *Bird at My Window*, appeared in 1966. Following the assassinations of black civil rights activists Malcolm X in 1964 and Martin Luther King, Jr., four years later, Guy traveled widely throughout the United States to study the effects of violence on the lives of young people. She published her findings in *Children of Longing*, which she edited in 1970.

Guy is best known for her novel *The Friends*, the first book in a trilogy that includes *Ruby* and *Edith Jackson*. In *The Friends*, Phyllisia Cathy discovers that her accent and ethnic background make her a target of ridicule among her peers after moving to Harlem from the West Indies. Phyllisia also confronts her own prejudices, particularly her embarrassment over the poverty of her best friend, Edith Jackson. *Ruby* focuses on Phyllisia's older sister, Ruby, who becomes increasingly alienated from the rest of her family during her teenage years.

In *Edith Jackson*, Guy returns to the character

of Edith Jackson, now a teenager, who struggles to hold her family together after the death of her father. While addressing the specific challenges of race and class that affect immigrants of African descent in the United States, Guy's trilogy also speaks to the broader issues of friendship, family, and personal responsibility that affect young people of all ethnic backgrounds. *The New York Times* selected *The Friends* as **Outstanding Book of the Year** for 1973.

In a second trilogy, which includes *The Disappearance*, *New Kids Around the Block*, and *And I Heard a Bird Sing*, Guy creates the compelling character of Imamu Jones. A quick and resourceful black teenager, Imamu Jones must rely on his street smarts and natural intelligence to survive in Harlem, where family tragedy, poverty, and violence constantly threaten to engulf him.

– Philip Bader

Harlem Writers Guild

The Harlem Writers Club was founded in 1950 by a group of black writers. (The name was later changed to the Harlem Writers Guild.) They had attended writer's workshops hosted by white writers and felt that, while their writing was appreciated, the whites did not appreciate the black life experience. The Guild was established to provide workshops with other black writers and encourage preserving the experiences of black people in writing and other creative arts. At mid-century, the struggle for equality was just beginning, and the Guild was also able to advance the movement for equal rights.

Margaret Peterson Haddix

Born: April 9, 1964; Washington Court House, Ohio

library.thinkquest.org/J0110073/author.html

Margaret Peterson Haddix is a versatile author who writes in various genres. She grew up surrounded by oral stories as a child. This led her to wanting to be a storyteller. However, she chose to write down her stories. She reported for newspapers before turning to writing young adult novels.

Haddix's first novel, *Running Out of Time*, is a mystery with a unique historical slant. Jessie Keyser lives in a Western frontier town in 1840. When an outbreak of diphtheria threatens the community, she learns that she is actually living in the 1990's and that her town is a modern-day tourist attraction that was created twelve years earlier as a scientific experiment. She escapes out to seek modern medical assistance for her dying younger sister, and although frightened by the strangeness of the modern world, accomplishes her mission.

Don't You Dare Read This, Mrs. Dunphrey, and *Leaving Fishers* are realistic fiction. Mrs. Dunphrey is an English teacher whose students keep journals to record ideas for other writings. She promises not to read her students's journals, until Tish pours out her problems in her journal and eventually allows the teacher to read it in order to get help. In *Leaving Fishers*, Dorry is pulled so fully into a religious cult that she

p.23

p.29

Diphtheria

Diphtheria is a very contagious bacterial infection that affects the respiratory system. Before a vaccine was developed and children were immunized with shots to prevent the disease, diphtheria caused many deaths in the young. The bacteria can be spread through the air or by physical contact. It causes a thick membrane to form over the throat, tonsils, and sinuses. A sore throat, cough, and fever results. The bacteria releases a poison into the system that can damage the heart, kidneys, and nervous system. Although it is rare in developed countries, diphtheria still kills about ten percent of those infected.

finds herself threatening dire consequences to the children she is babysitting if they do not convert along with her. This realization eventually moves her to extricate herself from the group.

Haddix moved to science fiction with *Among the Hidden*. In a **totalitarian** state that enforces a **two-children-only policy** with Population Police, Luke Garner is a third child who has spent his entire life in hiding. One day, he notices a shadowy figure in another house that he suspects is another person in hiding. This leads him to meet Jen and an entire network of hidden children who communicate via the Internet. In the sequel to this book, *Among the Imposters*, Luke becomes Lee Grant and is sent to a **boarding school** with terrifying consequences.

As in *Running Out of Time*, the novel *Turnabout* involves a science experiment gone awry. The story is set in 2085, when two elderly women reverse the aging process by taking a drug. As they become younger, they expect to be able to stop the process when they reach their ideal ages; however, they go all the way back to young childhood and must find someone to act as their parents, while trying to

521
p.300
.168

One-Child Policy

China put into action a one-child policy in 1979 to control the growth of the population. Parents in cities were allowed to have only one child. In the country, they could have two, but only if the first was a girl. Boy babies are preferred by Chinese. If a couple had more than one child, they were fined, taxed, and they did not receive free health care. Parents of one child received money from the state and free health care. Beginning in 1999, the Chinese government began to ease its one-child policy, feeling the population growth had been slowed.

avoid a reporter who has uncovered their experiment.

Just Ella is a continuation of the Cinderella fairy tale. Ella Brown plans to live happily ever after with her Prince Charming. However, her expectations quickly fade. Her soon-to-be husband proves to be boring, and she finds doing endless needlework dull. Ella decides that she cannot go through with her marriage, but her prince refuses to let her go. With the help of a servant girl, Ella escapes to seek a life where she is in charge.

Margaret Peterson Haddix has won a number of awards for her writing. *Just Ella*, *Don't You Dare Read This, Mrs. Dunphrey*, *Running Out of Time*, and *Among the Hidden* were all honored with American Library Association Best Books for Young Adults awards.

p.45

p.48

– Kay Moore

Mary Downing Hahn

Born: December 9, 1937; Washington, D.C.

www.childrensbookguild.org/hahn.html

Mary Downing Hahn is the author of many acclaimed young adult novels. Hahn's ability to create true-to-life characters who experience the real problems of growing up makes her books popular among young teenagers. Her books include historical fiction, suspense and horror, fantasy, and romance.

Hahn was born Mary Downing in Washington, D.C., and grew up in the nearby Baltimore area of Maryland. Her childhood in the 1940's and 1950's shaped the experiences that would eventually provide the backdrop for many of the small-town settings that give her books such an accurate sense of place and time. She began her professional career as a children's librarian in a public library system in Maryland. At the age of forty-one she became an author when her first book, *The Sara Summer*, was published in 1979.

Considered one of Hahn's most important novels, *Stepping on the Cracks*, is written from the perspective of a sixth-grader named Elizabeth whose brother is serving in World War II. Elizabeth and her best friend, Margaret, suddenly find themselves helping a neighborhood bully named Gordy save the life of his older brother. Hahn's gift for making settings seem real and characters come alive makes *Stepping on the Cracks* an exceptional book for young adult readers, and it won the prestigious Scott O'Dell Award for Historical Fiction.

Gordy's adventures continue in *Following My Own Footsteps* and *As Ever, Gordy*. An unlikely hero

p.117

p.87

p.35

p.51

TITLES

The Sara Summer, 1979

Daphne's Book, 1983

The Jellyfish Season, 1985

Wait Till Helen Comes, 1986

Tallahassee Higgins, 1987

December Stillness, 1988

Following the Mystery Man, 1988

The Dead Man in Indian Creek, 1990

The Spanish Kidnapping Disaster, 1991

Stepping on the Cracks, 1991

The Wind Blows Backwards, 1993

Time for Andrew, 1994

Look for Me by Moonlight, 1995

Following My Own Footsteps, 1996

The Gentleman Outlaw and Me—Eli, 1996

As Ever, Gordy, 1998

Promises to the Dead, 2000

Hear the Wind Blow, 2003

with many problems, Gordy and his family come from the wrong side of the tracks, and he earns a reputation as a bully. His mother and father eventually abandon him, but through it all Gordy manages to become like-able after he confronts a grand-mother, who expects the best from him, and an invalid neighbor boy, who shows him the true meaning of friendship.

Older teenagers are pulled into the drama of *The Wind Blows Back-wards*, a novel about a teenage girl's first love. In this story, a high school senior named Lauren falls in love with a boy who has a death wish. In an unusual coming-of-age story, Lauren is confronted with her boy-friend's behavior as he becomes increasingly **depressed** and erratic. In spite of tragic twists in the plot,

p.3

Teen Depression

About four percent of teens experience serious depression each year. The symptoms of depression are feeling sad for long periods of time, losing confidence in yourself, think-

ing life has no meaning, wanting to be alone, losing interest in hobbies and sports, being indeci-sive, changes in sleep patterns, feeling tired, and thinking about death or suicide. Depression can be treated by talking about it to a counselor, teacher, or parent. In addition to counseling, there are medicines that treat depression.

Dracula

Dracula is the title of the horror novel written by the Irish writer Bram Stoker and published in 1897. The story, told through journal entries and letters, tells of the vampire Count Dracula's attempt to spread his evil to London and his eventual defeat. It takes the ancient myth of the vampire and places it into a setting with characters and behavior that we now associate with the vampire story. Many stage play, film, and television portrayals of vampires owe much to the character created by Stoker.

readers find a hopeful and positive ending. Other books by Hahn dealing with real-life teenage problems include *Daphne's Book* and *The Jellyfish Season*.

Young adult readers appreciate Mary Downing Hahn's mysteries, thrillers, and ghost stories. In *Look for Me by Moonlight*, Cynda, a sixteen-year-old girl, confronts a **vampire**. In *Wait Till Helen Comes*, children in a blended family struggle to overcome the youngest child's upsetting secret—a secret she shares with a ghost. *Time for Andrew* is an interesting time travel fantasy in which two boys change places in time with an eerie conclusion.

p.303

– Grace Jasmine

Virginia Hamilton

Born: March 12, 1936; Yellow Springs, Ohio
Died: February 19, 2002; Dayton, Ohio

www.virginiahamilton.com/home.htm

An internationally acclaimed author of children's books and young adult fiction, **Virginia Hamilton** has explored numerous genres in her writing, including historical fiction, slave narratives, science fiction, fantasy, and mysteries. Her many literary honors include the **National Book Award**, the **Newbery Medal**, and the prestigious **Hans Christian Andersen Medal**.

Hamilton was born in a town near Dayton, Ohio. As a child, she was fascinated by the stories she heard from her parents about family ancestors, many of whom had escaped from slavery in the South and worked for the Underground Railroad. Hamilton excelled as a student and received a full **scholarship** to attend Antioch College. She later transferred to Ohio State University before moving to New York to study at the New School for Social Research. In 1960 she married poet Alfred Adoff, with whom she had two children. Meanwhile, she worked at odd jobs to help support her family and did her writing in her spare time.

Hamilton's first published book, *Zeely*, was inspired by her travels in Africa with her husband and won the **Nancy Block Memorial Award**. Hamilton followed this initial success with several **best-selling** children's books, including *The House of Dies Drear* and *The Time-Ago Tales of Jahdu*.

The Planet of Junior Brown depicts the life of a

p.117

p.122

p.380

p.384

p.8

p.10

p.25

p.305

shy, overweight eighth grader, Junior Brown, whose overbearing mother, Junella Brown, and eccentric piano teacher, Miss Peebs, contribute to his increasing emotional instability. With the help of a homeless youth, Buddy Clark, and a compassionate school janitor and former teacher, Mr. Pool, Junior eventually achieves some sense of normalcy in his life.

One of Hamilton's most successful works, *M. C. Higgins, the Great* is a coming-of-age story about a young man whose fight to preserve his family's ancestral home becomes the primary catalyst in his maturity from youth to manhood. *M. C. Higgins, the Great*, earned Hamilton the **National Book Award** and the American Library Association's **Newbery Medal**.

Hamilton published the first book in what has come to be called the Justice Cycle, *Justice and Her Brothers*, in 1978. This novel depicts the changes that occur in the life of the protagonist, Justice Douglass, and her brothers as they each realize that they have psychic powers that include telepathy, extrasensory perception, and the ability to travel in time. Hamilton continues their adventures in *Dustland*, which finds the Douglass siblings trapped in a bleak future world called Dustland. In *The Gathering*, the Douglass siblings must come together to protect the earth from impending evil.

732
p.45
.233
306
p.444

New School for Social Research

In 1919, a group of intellectuals founded the New School for Social Research in New York City. The mission of the school was to provide lifelong education to adults and to encourage thinking that would improve the world. The "University in Exile" was established in 1933 at the New School to provide a safe haven for newly exiled German scholars, victims of the rise of Adolf Hitler and the Nazi party. They contributed to the intellectual environment and helped make the New School a center for social science and contemporary arts in the 1930's and 1940's. The New School later acquired Parsons School of Design and the Actors Studio Drama School. Social science, humanities, and economic and public policy education are all featured in the school's curriculum.

In *Sweet Whispers, Brother Rush*, a fourteen-year-old girl, Tree Pratt, learns about the tragedies and triumphs of her family's past with the assistance of a supernatural guide, the ghost of her uncle Brother Rush. The knowledge she gains helps her make the difficult transition from adolescence to maturity. The novel was nominated for the **Before Columbus American Book Award** and won the Boston Globe-Horn Book Award, the Coretta Scott King Award, and the **Newbery Medal**.

p.747
p.6

Virginia Hamilton's published works for young adult readers span multiple genres. Whether she presents her tales in the form of science fiction, mystery, or fantasy, she consistently explores the themes of family, community, and racial heritage. In 1992 she received the **Hans Christian Andersen Award**—which has been called the "Little Nobel Prize"—for her contributions to young adult literature.

p.1

– Philip Bader

ESP

Extra**S**ensory **P**erception is the acquiring of information without using the senses or past experience. Telepathy is one type of ESP. We often refer to telepathy as mind reading or knowing someone's thoughts. Clairvoyance is knowing or sensing an object or an event that is far away in both time and place. We call this seeing into the past or the future. ESP is difficult to prove, and many scientists remain skeptical as to its existence. However, there are those who remain open to the possibility that evidence may someday support the existence of ESP.

Joyce Hansen

Born: October 18, 1942; New York, New York

www.joycehansen.com

An English and reading teacher in New York City schools for more than twenty years, **Joyce Hansen** has written books whose subjects range from early nineteenth century slaves to contemporary African Americans in inner cities. In all her work, she has drawn on her own students for inspiration. Known for her convincing depiction of African American children and their dialect, she writes in the hope that her students will relate to the topics within her books—recognizing the importance of family, holding on to hope, and living responsibly.

Hansen was born and reared in New York City. She lived in the Bronx with a mother who was passionate about books and reading and a photographer father who was passionate about sharing the beauty and poetry of his pictures, as well as the art of storytelling. Before becoming a school teacher, Hansen earned a bachelor's degree in English from Pace University and a master's degree in English education from New York University.

Hansen's first book, *Yellow Bird and Me*, concerns young African Americans in a contemporary inner-city environment. She continued their story fifteen years later in *One True Friend*. Meanwhile, she turned to historical fiction. *Which Way Freedom?* tells the story of a young slave, Obi, who joins an all-black Union regiment during the Civil War in order to acquire the freedom he fears he will acquire no other way. This book's sequel, *Out from This Place*, tells the story of Obi's female friend Easter, who becomes a free woman after the Civil War ends.

TITLES

Which Way Freedom?, 1986

Yellow Bird and Me, 1986

Out from This Place, 1988

The Captive, 1994

I Thought My Soul Would Rise and Fly: The Diary of Patsy, a Freed Girl, 1997

The Heart Calls Home, 1999

One True Friend, 2001

p.117

Gullah

"Gullah" refers to the group of African Americans who live on the sea islands and in the coastal areas of South Carolina, Georgia, and northeastern Florida, and whose ancestors were kidnapped from various African tribes and transported to the South to work the cotton plantations. These slaves were able to preserve elements of their African culture and develop a unique dialect, also called "Gullah," that combines African and English words and sounds. After emancipation, the Gullah stayed on the land and farmed. Gullah art, music and dance also demonstrate their African heritage. In the 1920's and 1930's, Julia Peterkin, a white plantation owner in South Carolina, learned their dialect and wrote stories about the Gullah that showed respect for their culture. She was criticized by fellow South Carolinians, but her novel *Scarlet Sister Mary* was awarded a Pulitzer Prize in 1928.

The Heart Calls Home finishes this trilogy, providing a realistic depiction of establishing a home in a black settlement called New Canaan. In all three books, Hansen includes authentic **Gullah** Island dialect with documented but little-known facts about the everyday lives of African Americans both before and after the Civil War.

p.30

I Thought My Soul Would Rise and Fly, part of Hansen's Dear America series, is a fictionalized diary of Patsy, a recently freed slave who is learning to live in the new post-Civil War order. *The Captive*, loosely based on an authentic early slave narrative, describes the passage of an **Ashanti** p.30 chieftain's son who is sold into slavery, transported from West Africa to America, and finally set free by Paul Cuffe, a black shipbuilder and captain.

Joyce Hansen's entire body of work is distinguished by her deep knowledge of the subjects she has researched and chosen to write about. Her narratives reveal great insight, balance, and substance. The complexity of history makes this challenging work, but Hansen relishes the opportunity to create books—whether contemporary or historical—that tell compelling stories while expanding their readers' perspectives. Hansen's writing honors include **Coretta Scott King Honor Book** awards for *Which Way Freedom?*, *The Captive*, and *I Thought My Soul Would Rise and Fly*.

p.66

– Alexa L. Sandmann

Ashanti

The small African state of Ashanti (now located in southern Ghana) grew into a wealthy and powerful empire through its participation in the European slave trade in the seventeenth to nineteenth centuries. The Ashantis provided Portuguese, British, French, Dutch, and other slave traders with captives obtained through warfare with neighboring states. These slaves were transported in ships and under inhumane conditions to the American continent via the deadly Middle Passage ocean route. The Akan people, who lived in Ashanti, also used the slave labor to mine gold and to clear forests for farming. In the late nineteenth century, the British established a presence in Ashanti. They looted much of the gold art preserved by the people, and it now can be seen in London at the British Museum.

Cynthia Harnett

Born: June 22, 1893; London, England
Died: October 25, 1981; London, England

Cynthia Harnett's success as a writer lies in the field of historical realism. She is meticulously accurate in historical details, yet still her writing gives imaginative lives to her main characters and their families. She is often compared to her contemporary Rosemary Sutcliff. The latter, however, wrote with a broader brush, and did not concentrate on late medieval and Elizabethan England in the ways Harnett did.

p.31

Harnett was born and reared in London, where she studied to be an artist at the Chelsea School of Art. During the 1930's and 1940's she collaborated with her artist-writer cousin, G. Vernon Stokes, in a series of books for young children about life in the country. Together, they produced a series of thirteen books with her text and his illustrations. Harnett continued to be an avid country lover all her life and also wrote several books about dogs.

p.3

In 1949 Harnett branched out on her own, writing *The Great House*, the story of an architect building a country house in the early eighteenth century. The focus on meticulous detail became typical of her subsequent historical work. This was followed in 1951 by *The Wool-Pack*, or *Nicholas and the Woolpack*, as it was titled in the United States (later still it was retitled *The Merchant's Mark*). This story is about the son of a sixteenth century wool merchant living in the sheep-producing region of the Cotswold Hills, some eighty miles west of London. Nicholas comes to London on his travels, and so Harnett is able to depict in a realistic way the sense of early Tudor England.

Elizabethan England

Elizabeth I was crowned Queen of England in 1558 when she was twenty five. She reigned until her death in 1603. She remained unmarried and was known as the Virgin Queen. Her reign was a period of political power and important cultural development. During her reign, Sir Francis Drake sailed around the globe between 1577 and 1580; the British defeated the Spanish Armada in 1588; and the East India Company, which would be a major catalyst for expanding the British Empire through international trade, was founded. Culturally, the awakening that had taken place in Italy earlier also occurred in England during the Elizabethan age. William Shakespeare is the most famous of the Elizabethan poets and playwrights.

Harnett's book, *The Drawbridge Gate*, is perhaps better suited for children than young adults, being the true story of Dick Whittington, who for a time was mayor of London in the late fourteenth and early fifteenth centuries. Harnett is careful to separate fact from the fantasy that has mythologized this figure, and this is where young adult interest might come into play. For example, Harnett researched some of the bomb sites of post-World War II central London, even making some original archaeological finds.

p.83

Harnett's later books include *Stars of Fortune* about the English ancestry of George Washington, the first president of the United States. *Caxton's Challenge* is set in late fifteenth century London and concerns the rivalry between the first printers and the professional handwriters, or scriveners, of the day. Harnett gives detailed descriptions of the printing process.

Harnett illustrated all of her own young adult fiction books except the last, *The Writing on the Hearth*, which took her ten years to research. This

Battle of Agincourt

The Hundred Years' War was waged by the King Henry V of England against the French. He was determined to capture all of France. This battle, fought in northeastern France in 1415, was the most important military battle in the late Middle Ages. It marked the beginning of a string of victories for the English. In 1420, Henry became the heir to the crown of France. The French had chosen a poor site for the battle and had limited experience with English archery. This battle symbolized the transition from an age of knighthood to one of a disciplined infantry using modern weapons.

novel is set in an Oxfordshire village during the early fifteenth century, in King Henry V's time shortly after the **Battle of Agincourt**. However, it is not about high politics but deals with a young lad who wants to become an Oxford scholar, but who gets involved in treason and witchcraft instead.

p.31

p.42

Cynthia Harnett's second young adult novel, *Nicholas and the Woolpack*, won her Britain's prestigious **Carnegie Medal** in 1951. *Caxton's Challenge* made the honors list for the 1959 **Carnegie Medal**.

– David Barratt

James S. Haskins

Born: September 19, 1941; Demopolis, Alabama

www.childrenslit.com/f_haskins.html

James S. Haskins is a prolific, award-winning writer of books for children and young adults about African American history and biography. His early books dealt with social issues such as teenage **alcoholism**, street gangs, child abuse, and rights of the **disabled** as well as black political and cultural figures. His history books focus mostly on the Civil War era and the **Civil Rights movement**. He has also written many biographies about sports figures, entertainers, and world leaders.

Born in Alabama and reared in the still-**segregated** South, Haskins wanted to read books from an early age but was denied use of the local public library because he was black. His mother got him some reading material in a grocery store that offered encyclopedia volumes at special prices. After Haskins finished high school, he took part in the Civil Rights movement and met Martin Luther King, Jr. He later became a school teacher and drew on his experience in a **Harlem** school to write his first book, *Diary of a Harlem Schoolteacher* (1969), an autobiographical work. After he published that book, his publishers suggested that he write for young adults.

While most of Haskins's writ-

TITLES

The Headless Haunt and Other African-American Ghost Stories, 1994

Moaning Bones: African-American Ghost Stories, 1998

ings are nonfiction, and it is for these works that he has won various literary awards, he does have several fictional books which expand his exploration of the African American heritage. *The Headless Haunt and Other African-American Ghost Stories* includes more than twenty tales drawn from the oral tradition as well as stories that were recorded by members of the Georgia Writers' Project during the 1930's. These chilling stories were passed from generation to generation in the South. His introduction to the book explains how African American folklore blends aspects of African culture with elements of life in the new land. The stories are divided by the types of ghost each story depicts.

▶ p.315

Moaning Bones: African-American Ghost Stories continues Haskins's retelling of African American tales. This book contains seventeen spooky stories, which, like those in his earlier book,

Americans with Disabilities Act

In 1990, Congress passed the Americans with Disabilities Act (ADA), giving some forty-three million Americans with disabilities broad civil rights. The ADA protects people with both physical and mental disabilities that limit life activities. It prohibits discrimination against the disabled in employment, public services, and public accommodations. Some of theses accommodations include making communication devices available to those with blindness, speech, or hearing problems; providing access for those in wheelchairs to office buildings, parks, sports facilities, libraries, and public transportation; and requiring employers to reconsider how they evaluate applicants for jobs. The ADA offers people with all types of disabilities an opportunity to take a greater part in public life.

AMERICANS WITH DISABILITIES ACT: EXPANDING OPPORTUNITIES

Georgia Writers' Project

When Franklin Delano Roosevelt was elected president in 1932, the country was in the midst of the Great Depression and many people were out of work. As part of FDR's New Deal, he created the Works Progress Administration (WPA) to create jobs. One part of this program was the Federal Writers' Project, to which the Georgia Writers' Project (GWP) belonged. The GWP hired out-of-work people to interview former slaves who were still living in Georgia and to write down their life stories. The Folklore Project was also established to gather folklore through interviews with Georgians. These projects collected valuable information from many elderly Georgians that would have been lost forever.

came out of the work done in Georgia. Readers may recognize "Ghost in the Backseat" as similar to the favorite campfire story about a scary hitchhiker. Other tales visit a haunted steamship, the "big house" of a plantation, and the Lake of the Dead.

James S. Haskins is a professor of English at the University of Florida in Gainesville and a member of the board of *Footsteps*, a magazine about African American history which may be found in many schools. His recent nonfiction publications include *Toni Morrison: Telling a Tale Untold* (2002) and *Champion: The Story of Muhammad Ali* (2002).

– Kay Moore

Erik Christian Haugaard

Born: April 13, 1923; Frederiksberg, Denmark

Both critics and young people love **Erik Christian Haugaard**'s vivid characters and settings. His books feature teenage boys who live during wartime, deal with as many traitors as friends, and make difficult decisions as they learn to survive. His adult characters are frequently cruel, though a few are always admirable and lovable. Haugaard makes distant places and times seem vibrant and colorful.

Haugaard was a teenager on a Danish farm when German troops invaded his country in 1940. He then fled to the United States and attended college in North Carolina. He served in the Royal Canadian Air Force during World War II, attended school in New York, and worked as a shepherd in Wyoming before he published his first book, *Hakon of Rogen's Saga*, which received an American Library Association **Notable Book Award**. Soon he was writing a new book almost every year.

p.4

Haugaard set *Hakon of Rogen's Saga* in Norway during the Viking era. After young Hakon's father, Olaf, marries pretty Thora against her father's will, her father sends an army against the small land of Rogen. Olaf's cruel brother Sigurd refuses to help him but after Olaf is killed in battle, he takes control of Rogen and tries to murder Hakon. The boy hides out in a cave and learns to hunt and feed himself while planning his revenge.

Orphans of the Wind tells of Jim, a twelve-year-old English orphan, who is sold by his uncle to work on the ship *Four Winds*. Jim learns about both seamanship and human nature as the ship sails to

America, but when he and three friends are shipwrecked in the midst of the American Civil War, they are forced to choose between joining Confederate slavers or fighting for the Union.

Slavery, injustice, and poverty are major themes in Haugaard's work. *The Little Fishes* describes a twelve-year-old beggar in wartime Italy, his daily search for food and for the meaning of life, and how he learns compassion that helps him survive. In *The Rider and His Horse*, a boy is one of the seven Jewish survivors of Masada during the fall of ancient Jerusalem. Set in the American Revolution, *A Boy's Will* describes how Patrick defies his cruel grandfather by warning the American naval captain John Paul Jones that the English plan to ambush him.

p.317

Haugaard also wrote many exciting books set in Japan. In *The Samurai's Tale*, orphaned Taro grows up as a samurai fighting

347

Masada

In 63 B.C.E., the Romans occupied Israel. In time, a group of Israeli rebels attempted to overthrow Roman rule. This rebellion continued until the Great Revolt from 66 C.E. through 70 C.E., when the Romans finally conquered Jerusalem and destroyed the Second Temple. A group of 960 rebels fled the city to the hilltop Roman fortress at Masada, an enormous and isolated rock that rose up above the Dead Sea. For three years the band of rebels (men, women, and children) held off the attacking Romans, who remained camped at the base of Masada. Finally, as Roman success seemed near, the rebel leaders called upon all members of the group to commit suicide, rather than submit to the enemy. Only two women and five children survived the mass suicide. Suicide is forbidden by the Jewish religion so this was a bold decision. This event in Jewish history was long forgotten until 1920 when a poem was written celebrating the event. Since then, Masada has become an important symbol to Jewish people and one of the most visited sites in Israel.

for the enemies of his dead family. In *The Boy and the Samurai*, the orphan Saru helps a samurai rescue his wife from a warlord amid a civil war. *The Revenge of the Forty-seven Samurai* tells of a fourteen-year-old surrounded by treachery as his master assembles a team to avenge Lord Asano's death.

p.17
Erik Christian Haugaard is famous for his translations of fairy tales by the nineteenth century Danish writer **Hans Christian Andersen**. He p.31 also wrote fairy tales of his own, such as *Prince Boghole*, in which an Irish king promises his daughter's hand to the prince who brings him the most p.747 wonderful bird. Haugaard's many writing honors include a Boston Globe-Horn Book Award for *The Little Fishes* and a Phoenix Award for *The Rider* p.14 *and his Horse.*

– Fiona Kelleghan

Hans Christian Andersen

Hans Christian Andersen is known for his famous collections of fairy tales written between 1832 and 1875. As a poor young boy, he had heard stories from his grandmother in Denmark. He was ambitious and eventually became a writer and travelled throughout Europe, making friends with important people in the arts and with the royal families of Europe. He added to his grandmother's stories the folktales he heard on his travels. Soon his tales were well known in Germany, Holland, and England. Andersen died in 1875, but his books have never been out of print.

Nathaniel Hawthorne

Born: July 4, 1804; Salem, Massachusetts
Died: May 19, 1864; Plymouth, New Hampshire
www.kirjasto.sci.fi/hawthorn.htm

Nathaniel Hawthorne is one of America's outstanding literary figures. A pioneer in the development of American literature, he wrote books that were popular in his day and that have been studied by serious students of literature and scholars ever since. His books tend to have American settings and treat important eras in American history.

Hawthorne was born and reared in Salem, Massachusetts, a New England city famous for its **witch trials** during the colonial era. During the early 1820's he attended **Bowdoin College** in Maine, where he became a close friend of Franklin Pierce, the future president of the United States. After finishing college, Hawthorne held a number of political appointments, including surveyor of customs at the Salem Custom House, where he claimed he got the idea for *The Scarlet Letter*, and which serves as the setting of that book's preface, entitled "The Custom House." When Pierce ran for the presidency in 1852, Hawthorne wrote his official campaign biography. When Hawthorne died twelve years later, he was trying to regain his health while traveling with Pierce.

Hawthorne was also a friend of the philosopher and essayist Ralph Waldo Emerson, Henry David Thoreau, the author of *Walden* (1854),

.446

 p.320

TITLES

Twice-Told Tales, 1837

The Scarlet Letter, 1850

The House of the Seven Gables, 1851

Salem Witchcraft Trials

In 1692, a group of young Puritan girls from Salem Village, Massachusetts, began meeting secretly to listen to the voodoo-like tales of a slave from Barbados. Before long, the girls started behaving strangely, complaining of illnesses, trembling, babbling, and going into trances. To the Puritan community, this was a sign that the Devil was at work. When pressured to talk about the source of their frightening behavior, the girls charged the slave and two other women with witchcraft. More accusations followed. On June 8, the first accused witch went to the gallows. By September 22, twenty convicted witches had been hanged. The citizens of the surrounding counties began to challenge the courts in the witchcraft trials. By May, 1693, all remaining imprisoned "witches" were released and the infamous witchcraft trials ended.

and Herman Melville, who was best known for his novel *Moby Dick* (1851), which he dedicated to Hawthorne. In 1842 Hawthorne married Sophia Peabody. They had two children, including a son named Julian, who became a novelist himself.

Hawthorne wrote many stories for children but aimed most of his works at adults. He wrote many important short stories and romances, novel-length works in which, he felt, he could introduce elements of the supernatural.

Critics hail *The Scarlet Letter* as one of the masterpieces of American literature. Set in the 1650's, it is the story of Hester Prynne, a married woman who commits adultery with the Reverend Arthur Dimmesdale and gives birth to a daughter named Pearl. Hester's husband, who calls himself Roger Chillingworth, comes to Salem just as Hester and her daughter are exposed on the scaffold with Hester wearing a scarlet letter *A* (for "adultery") embroidered on her garment. Set in the **Puritan New England** of Hawthorne's ancestors, the romance traces the lives,

p.638

both interior and exterior, of the central characters as they face their destinies.

The House of the Seven Gables is set in Hawthorne's own time. It deals with the Pyncheon family, whose members seem unable to escape from a curse that had been laid on the family generations earlier by one of the Maules. Judge Jaffrey Pyncheon frames Clifford Pyncheon for what is believed to be a murder. When Clifford gets out of jail, he returns to live in a place known as the House of the Seven Gables with Hepzibah Pyncheon. A boarder in the house, Holgrave, is a descendant of the Maules. Whatever hope there is for the happiness of the Pyncheon family lies in Phoebe, a cousin from the country, with whom Holgrave falls in love.

p.321

Considered a giant of American literature, Hawthorne explores American themes in American settings. As his friend Melville recognized, Hawthorne helped establish an American literature distinctly different from the literature of England.

– Richard Tuerk

House of the Seven Gables

The actual house that inspired Nathaniel Hawthorne to write *The House of the Seven Gables* is located in Salem, Massachusetts. Also known as the Turner-Ingersoll Mansion, it was built in 1668 and is the oldest surviving seventeenth century wooden mansion in New England. The house is on the National Register of Historic Places and is open to the public as a museum. The house where Hawthorne was born was moved to the site in Salem and is also open to the public for viewing.

Ernest Hemingway

Born: July 21, 1899; Oak Park, Illinois
Died: July 2, 1961; Ketchum, Idaho

www.lostgeneration.com/hrc.htm

TITLES

In Our Time, 1924, 1925

A Farewell to Arms, 1929

The Old Man and the Sea, 1952

Because of his compelling prose style and his vision of heroism, **Ernest Hemingway** holds a secure place among the leading fiction writers of the twentieth century. His works, which have often been the basis for successful films, retain their appeal to a large reading public and to students of literature. The most pervasive element of his writing is his development of a hero whose values are clear, who lives by a code, and who is doomed to defeat despite his efforts.

Born into an affluent family in Illinois, Ernest Hemingway always courted adventure. During World War I, he volunteered to become a front-line Red Cross ambulance driver in Italy, where he was wounded and hospitalized. Returning home a hero, he recuperated at his family's summer place in northern Michigan.

In 1921 Hemingway and his wife, Hadley Richardson, moved to Paris, where they mingled with many American expatriate writers, including Gertrude Stein, F. Scott Fitzgerald, and Ezra Pound. They lived on Hadley's trust income and on the pittance the *Toronto Star* paid Hemingway as a foreign correspondent. Hemingway's stories did not sell well at that time, but his collection *In Our Time* was printed in a small edition and later in a larger edition. Well received critically, it launched Hemingway's writing career.

In Our Time consists of fourteen interrelated stories, eight of which focus on Nick Ad-

p.323

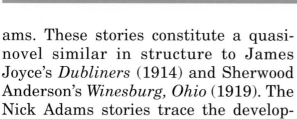

Gertrude Stein

Gertrude Stein was a wealthy American writer who lived most of her life in France. Her home in Paris, located at 27 rue de Fleurus, became a gathering place for writers, artists, and composers. In addition to Ernest Hemingway, she also hosted artists Picasso and Matisse, as well as American composer Virgil Thompson. From 1907 until her death in 1946, Stein lived with her friend and lover Alice B. Toklas. Her writing was experimental, and she is appreciated for her use of language.

ams. These stories constitute a quasi-novel similar in structure to James Joyce's *Dubliners* (1914) and Sherwood Anderson's *Winesburg, Ohio* (1919). The Nick Adams stories trace the development of Nick from childhood to adulthood and are set, in part, in the region of northern Michigan where Hemingway's family had a summer home. Hemingway's collection contains brief interchapters on the violence he experienced in World War I, in the Graeco-Turkish War—which he covered as a correspondent—and at bullfights in Spain. The unifying thread in these stories is temporal rather than physical, as it was in Joyce's and Anderson's novels.

Hemingway's *A Farewell to Arms* is regarded as one of the finest novels ever written about World War I. Its protagonist, Lieutenant Frederic Henry, is injured and, during his recovery in an Italian hospital, falls in love with and impregnates his nurse, Catherine Barkley. He is then sent back to the battlefront. However, during the retreat from Caporetto, he deserts and reunites with Catherine. The lovers flee to neutral Switzerland, where they spend several idyllic months before Catherine delivers a stillborn child, then dies from a hemorrhage. Hemingway's pessimistic conclusion is that war thwarts love and negates human tenderness.

The Hemingway novel most frequently read in

p.233

Hemingway in Cuba

Cuba became Ernest Hemingway's home away from home in 1932. At the time, Cuba was a playground for America's rich. It also appealed to Hemingway because of his love of deep-sea fishing. In 1940, he bought *Finca Vigia* (Lookout Farm) a fifteen acre property about fifteen miles from Havana. He made *Finca Vigia* his home, even staying on after Castro came to power in 1959. His health declining, Hemingway left Cuba in 1960. His house is now a government museum, and his fishing boat *Pilar* is on display there. Some of the Cubans who worked for Hemingway remain as caretakers of the property.

secondary schools is *The Old Man and the Sea*, which deals with quest and with the disappointment and disillusionment that frequently accompany the fulfillment of a quest. The brief and tightly controlled story is about Santiago, a **Cuban** fisherman, and his young helper, Manolin. Santiago goes for eighty-four days without catching a fish. Manolin brings him food and tries to elevate his spirits, but Santiago is severely depressed. Santiago's fishing line finally becomes taut when he goes out alone in his skiff. He has snagged a huge marlin, the largest he has ever seen. As he struggles to land the fish, the two engage in a mortal struggle for three days and three nights. The old man, near death from exhaustion, finally lands the noble fish and brings it arduously to shore. However, by the time he lands his boat, sharks have torn away most of the marlin's flesh. The prize the old man brings in is little more than a skeleton.

p.32

The Old Man and the Sea brought Hemingway his only **Pulitzer Prize** in 1953. The work was influential in securing for him the **Nobel Prize in Literature** the following year.

p.137

p.23

– R. Baird Shuman

Hermann Hesse

Born: July 2, 1877; Calw, Germany
Died: August 9, 1962; Montagnola, Switzerland

www.hermann-hesse.de/eng

Hermann Hesse's fiction has experienced two waves of popularity. His books were first popular among German-speaking youths during the early part of the twentieth century. Almost amazingly, he once again became a cult favorite, in translation, among American college students during the 1960's, during which his books sold more than ten million copies in the United States alone. During this same period, Hesse also was popular in other countries, such as Japan and Sweden. The primary reason for his extraordinary popularity among the youth of the world can be traced to the fact that his novels focus primarily on youthful central characters who are in search for the meaning of life in a chaotic world.

Hesse was born in Calw, Germany. His father was a missionary and his mother the daughter of a missionary. Although Hesse studied to become a missionary himself, he became distraught with the formal education that he was receiving and vowed to become a writer. He came to believe that his authoritarian **school system** only bred mediocrity and that "genius" could only flourish outside of this system.

In 1904 Hesse published his first novel, *Peter Camenzind*. It depicts a Swiss youth who needs to escape from the village of his birth in order to find adventure and enlightenment. *Peter Camenzind* was a literary success and foreshadowed many of the themes that Hesse would revisit in his later novels. Hesse also married his first wife, Maria Bernoulli, in 1904. They settled in the Swiss town of Gaien-hofen, located on Lake Constance. At his idyllic

326▶

TITLES

Peter Camenzind, 1904

Beneath the Wheel, 1906 (also known as *The Prodigy*)

Demian, 1919

Siddhartha, 1922

Steppenwolf, 1927

Narcissus and Goldmund, 1930 (also known as *Death and the Lover*)

The Journey to the East, 1932

The Glass Bead Game, 1943 (also known as *Magister Ludi*)

home, Hesse was able to concentrate on writing his novels.

In Hesse's next book, *Beneath the Wheel*, he examined an educational system that he himself knew all too well. The novel has been called Hesse's spiritual autobiography. The character of Hans Giebenrath is a scholar and is the pride of his German town. At school he meets another student, Hermann, who is a "free poetic soul." Hans is shattered by the realization of what the German bourgeois society expects of him. Hermann can escape society's brutality by being creative, but Hans seems destined to end up "beneath the wheel" of the inhumane system.

Demian is Hesse's first post-World War I novel. Its **protagonist** and narrator, Emil Sinclair, is a youth who must find his place in the world. The novel's sensitive portrayal of a youth wrestling with issues of self-discovery helped to make it popular among young German World War I veterans. The young

p.23

German School System

The German school system of Hesse's youth was governed by the Prussian code of discipline. Students attended the lower school where learning required memorization of facts and even passages from literature. Independent thinking was not encouraged. Students were evaluated early in their schooling and directed into one of three tracks: apprenticeship and labor, trade school and business or government office work, or university and a profession. The modern German school system more closely resembles the American model.

India

Hesse called *Siddhartha* "an Indic Poem." Of all his fiction, it is the one work that depends most on Indian religion and philosophy. Hesse acknowledged his interest in India and his fascination with Hinduism, Buddhism, Vedanta, and Yoga. India had been his family's spiritual homeland for two generations, and he had taken a voyage to India in 1911. *Siddhartha* was his artistic expression of his understanding of the Indian view of life. In the 1950's to the 1970's, many Western young people discovered Hesse's work. Its message of disinterested love appealed to America's "flower children" and attracted many young people to Eastern religions and philosophy.

protagonist of the novel takes inspiration from the Christlike figure of Max Demian, who befriends the young Emil.

Hesse used *Siddhartha* to write about a spiritual journey. Siddhartha is a young Indian from the sixth century B.C.E. who struggles to find spiritual peace of mind. Always fascinated with Eastern religious philosophies, Hesse borrowed from the inspired life of the Buddha himself to flesh out his moral tale. The quest for spiritual and/or psychological growth is at the center of Hesse's most noteworthy novels, including *Steppenwolf, Narcissus and Goldmund, The Journey to the East*, and *The Glass Bead Game*.

Hermann Hesse was awarded the Nobel Prize in Literature in 1946, and he still ranks as one of the major world novelists of his time.

– Jeffry Jensen

Karen Hesse

Born: August 29, 1952; Baltimore, Maryland

www.kidsreads.com/authors/au-hesse-karen.asp

Karen Hesse placed her first young adult novel, *Out of the Dust*, in a historical setting, the tragic Dust Bowl of the 1930's. The novel is divided into sections by the seasons of the year and is told in an innovative, diary-like verse form. *Out of the Dust* and *Witness* both contain many of the same elements: underprivileged families, young adults called upon to act maturely and responsibly in a time of crisis, and realistic settings.

p.11

Born in Maryland, Hesse was often ill when she was a child. She felt out of place in her surroundings and sought the comfort of reading for hours at a time while perched in a tree or visiting the library. A book that was especially important to her was John Hersey's *Hiroshima* (1946), which tells the stories of six survivors of the first atomic bomb the United States dropped on Japan in World War II. Hesse was so inspired by the courage of Hersey's characters that she credits his book with lifting her out of her childhood.

p.467

Another thing Hesse did as a child was ride with her father when he made his rounds as a collection agent. That experience made her aware of the difficulties faced by families in serious financial trouble. As she grew older, her vivid imagination led to her success in high school drama; however, she gave up theater midway through college when she married. She began writing and working in the school library when she returned to finish her degree.

Hesse's first published novels appeal mostly to pre-adolescent readers. They feature strong characters facing challenges of catastrophic proportions. Especially notable are *Letters from Rifka* (1992), set in post-revolutionary Russia, and *Phoenix Rising* (1994), set in a fictional post-nuclear war society.

Out of the Dust is Hesse's first young adult novel. Its central character is an adolescent girl who writes a poetic journal describing how she and her family are struggling to save their farm from being taken away by a bank because of unpaid loans. Along with dust storms, a horrendous kitchen fire adds to their problems. The fire damages the narrator's hands so severely that she can no longer play her beloved piano. Healing is slow for the girl, her family, and the land. The story is unusually dark for its genre yet proves fascinating to young adults.

The Dust Bowl

In the 1930's, the combination of bad agricultural practices and a long drought turned the southern plains of the U.S. into a dust bowl. Grasslands had been plowed and planted with wheat. When drought and then winds came, there was nothing to hold the soil. Winds blew dust, turning the sky dark for days at a time. Acres of agricultural land became useless and thousands of people were forced to leave their homes. The states of Kansas, Texas, Colorado, New Mexico, and Oklahoma were hardest hit. Those who left for places such as California were often called "Okies" because so many of them arrived from Oklahoma.

KAREN HESSE

Witness, also written in verse form, is set in Vermont during a 1924 outbreak of **Ku Klux Klan** activity. Hesse uses a variety of characters to describe the growing Klan influence as events in a small town build to explosive proportions. This shifting point-of-view technique reveals how racial prejudice can sometimes be rationalized. Portrait photographs in the front of the book help readers to visualize characters. As racism reaches its extreme, a young Klan member is assigned to poison the well of a black family. Hesse adds power to the narrative by contrasting the feverish activity in the town with the serenity of its natural setting.

Karen Hesse's writing awards include the **Newbery Medal** and the Scott O'Dell Award for Historical Fiction for *Out of the Dust*. *Witness* won the **Christopher Award**, which recognizes works that promote positive values.

– Margaret A. Dodson

p.33
p.102
p.5

Ku Klux Klan

The Ku Klux Klan (KKK) was first established in 1866 to keep newly free African Americans from voting. Clan members came mostly from the ranks of the former Confederate Army. They dressed in masks, cardboard hats, and draped themselves in white sheets. They harrassed blacks, set fires, or killed blacks and their white supporters. Soon they expanded their harrassment to black businesses. Following World War I, they added Jews, Roman Catholics, socialists, communists, and immigrants to their list of enemies. By 1944, the Klan was disbanded. However, with the rise of the Civil Rights movement in the 1950's the Klan was reborn. Clan members were responsible for much of the opposition and murder that occurred throughout the year's of struggle for African Americans' civil rights.

Jamake Highwater

Born: 1930's?; place unknown
Died: June 3, 2001; Los Angeles, California

www.nypl.org/research/chss/spe/rbk/faids/
highwatr.html #biog

Jamake Highwater is best known for his work on Native American culture in a variety of art forms. His novels include compelling and universal themes of loss of identity, the disintegration of the family and culture due to poverty, alcoholism, and rejection of traditional values.

Highwater's birthplace and even the date of his birth are unknown. His Native American parents left him at an orphanage. He was adopted when he was about seven years old and was raised in Southern California. The image of a young man cut off from his culture, recovering his identity through Native American legend and art, is present throughout Highwater's life and his art.

Highwater's novel *Anpao: An American Odyssey* has been widely acclaimed as exceptional in its expression of the American Indian viewpoint, particularly in its blending of history and mysticism. The novel is rich with traditional Native American tales woven together to form the adventures of Anpao, a brave young hero who journeys through time and space from the legendary world of his ancestors to encounters with the white man.

Legend Days, *The Ceremony of Innocence*, and *I Wear the Morning Star* make up Highwater's Ghost Horse Cycle. *Legend Days* is the story of Amana, a young girl who is orphaned by a smallpox epidemic. She witnesses famine, the invasion of white settlers, and the near-extinction of the Plains tribes in the late nineteenth century. Amana is a determined survivor and a brave heroine. The first book ends with

TITLES

Anpao: An American Odyssey, 1977

The Sun, He Dies, 1980

Legend Days, 1984

The Ceremony of Innocence, 1985

I Wear the Morning Star, 1986

p.332

Smallpox

This highly contagious disease is caused by the variola virus. Before modern medicine, up to one third of smallpox victims died of the disease. Science, however, put a stop to smallpox by the discovery of a vaccine that makes people immune to the virus. Edward Jenner, an English doctor who lived from 1749-1832, noticed that dairy workers who had been exposed to cowpox did not become infected with smallpox. Cowpox proved to be a similar virus that was harmless to humans. Vaccination with cowpox created immunity to smallpox in humans. From 1967 through 1980, the World Health Organization waged a worldwide campaign of early detection, isolation, and vaccination. This wiped out the disease and the last reported case was in 1980.

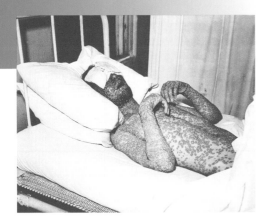

the death of her beloved husband Far Away Son, who is her link with the traditions of her people.

In *The Ceremony of Innocence*, Amana finds brief happiness with a French Canadian trader, but he leaves her before their daughter Jemina is born. Amana is deeply distressed that she cannot teach Jemina the old ways. Her daughter marries Jamie Ghost Horse, a rodeo performer and movie stuntman, who is modeled on Highwater's own father. Jemina and Jamie have two sons. Reno, the eldest, wants nothing but to be a typical American boy, but the youngest son, Sitko, is the boy Amana knows will remember the old ways she teaches him. The novel ends sadly as Amana, an old woman, gives up the grandsons she has raised so that their mother can take them to a boarding school.

I Wear the Morning Star shifts to the voice of Sitko. As Highwater himself was, Sitko is abandoned at a foster home by his mother and becomes a sad outsider. He begins to paint the memories and images that he cannot forget. Eventually he is adopted and discovers himself as an artist. The legends live in his images. Despite difficulties and the clash of cultures, Sitko and the legends survive.

p.1

p.1

YOUNG ADULT AUTHORS

Jamake Highwater was honored by the **Black-feet Indian** tribe for his achievements as an **interpreter** of Native American culture. The numerous awards for his books, which are popular with both children and adults, include **Newbery Honor Book** and **Boston Globe-Horn Honor Book** awards for *Anpao*. He has also written nonfiction about Native American art, dance, and mythology, and produced television documentaries on Native American culture.

– Susan Butterworth

333

 p.17

p.102

p.747

Blackfeet Confederacy

The Blackfeet Confederacy consisted of four Algonquian Indian tribes: the Siksika, Kainah, Northern Piegan, and Southern Piegan. They originally came from somewhere in the east and had a common language and similar religious beliefs. They lived in the Northern Plains, with the largest populations in Montana and Alberta, Canada. Geography separated the tribes, especially in the mountains. Each branch of the Confederacy lived in a separate valley or along a different river. The Blackfeet came together to fight invaders, to hunt for food, and to celebrate weddings and successful hunts. The tribes moved about frequently in search of the American bison, their main source of food and clothing.

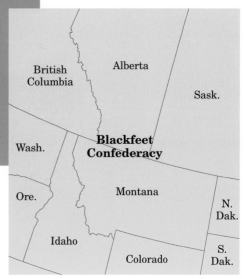

Tony Hillerman

Born: May 27, 1925; Sacred Heart, Oklahoma

www.tonyhillermanbooks.com

Tony Hillerman is best known for his anthropological mysteries, which have garnered him several awards, including the Spur Award of the Western Writers of America for the best novel set in the West for *Skinwalkers*. His unique mysteries, most of which are set on the Navajo Reservation in the Southwest, contain masterful interactions among the characters, settings, and plots. Although Hillerman's novels are written primarily for adults, their suspense, mystery, and supernatural elements appeal equally strongly to young adults.

Born in Oklahoma, Hillerman had contacts with Native Americans throughout his life. In his youth, he lived among Indians in Oklahoma. When he returned to the United States after being wounded in World War II, he observed a curing ceremony for Navajo members of the Marines on the Navajo Reservation in 1945. His college education in Oklahoma and New Mexico and later employment at the University of New Mexico gave him the opportunity to learn more about Native Americans, especially the Navajo.

The driving force behind each of Hillerman's mysteries is a set of characters who become immersed in the classic conflict of

p.33

p.72

p.2

The Western Writers of America established the prestigious Spur Awards in 1953. They annually select winners in a number of categories of Western literature. Awards are presented for best western novel (short), best novel of the west (long), best original paperback novel, best short story, best short nonfiction, best contemporary nonfiction, best bigraphy, best history, best juvenile fiction, best juvenile nonfiction, best television or motion picture drama, best television or motion picture documentary, and best first novel.

good versus evil against the mythic, spiritual landscape of the Southwest. Joe Leaphorn and Jim Chee are both tribal police officers who move between and function in two worlds: the white, urban, fast-paced world and the mythic, spiritual world of the Navajo. They know that any crime—but especially violent crime—upsets the cosmic order, the harmony inherent in all things. To reestablish order and return the land and its people to harmony, they must eradicate the evil. By relying on their analytical powers and their knowledge of Navajo spiritualism, they solve the mysteries.

In *The Blessing Way*, Hillerman's first novel, Leaphorn discovers a corpse with a mouthful of sand in the Many Ruins Canyon. He attempts to solve the mysterious murder by tracking a supernatural killer known as "Wolf Witch." Again, in *Listening Woman*, Leaphorn investigates a murder involving witches and ghosts. He solves the mystery because he understands his people and the cold-blooded killers who have been committing heinous crimes against humanity. Hillerman's next three novels, *People of Darkness*, *The Dark Wind* and *The Ghostway*, develop the character of Jim Chee, who is studying to become a singer, a **shaman** who conducts healing rituals. Chee uses his knowledge of Navajo rituals, **sorcery**, and cleansing rituals to solve the murders.

Shaman

A Native American tribe's medical practioner was the shaman, a man or woman who had acquired supernatural healing powers through a number of rituals, a vision quest, a dream, by receiving a sign, through inheritance, by surviving an illness, or through resurrection after "death." The supernatural power could be general or specific to certain illnesses. Shamans maintained their power through frequent rituals such as sweating, dreaming, reciting curing songs, isolation, fasting, and purifying their medicines and tools. Shamans were respected and sometimes feared. A person who cured could also be a sorcerer. Today, many Indian Health Service facilities combine Western medical treatment with the activities of a traditional tribal shaman.

Hillerman brings his two detectives together in *Skinwalkers* and *A Thief of Time* and subsequent novels to confront villains who subvert the cosmic order of nature and create terror and violence. In both novels, the villains commit crimes because they have allowed greed or pride to overcome their conscience. Leaphorn and Chee solve the crimes and restore the natural order.

All of Tony Hillerman's novels begin in a suspenseful fashion: one of the **protagonist's** lives is threatened, a person disappears under a suspicious set of circumstances, or dead bodies are discovered. Against this backdrop are the supernatural beliefs of the Navajos, which are germane to the plot. Because Leaphorn and Chee understand these beliefs, they are able to solve the crimes in a logical, analytical fashion.

p.2

– Sharon K. Wilson and Raymond Wilson

S. E. Hinton

Born: July 22, 1948; Tulsa, Oklahoma

www.sehinton.com

84 ▶

Most of **best-selling** novelist **S. E. Hinton**'s characters are realistically drawn adolescent boys who have serious problems. With parents who are typically absent, **alcoholic**, or dead, the boys rely on brothers or close male friends for strength and support. Usually living on the wrong side of the tracks, they belong to gangs and often get in fights and have trouble with police. Death, poverty, drugs, and prejudice dominate their daily lives.

101 ▶

Born Susan Eloise Hinton in Tulsa, Oklahoma, Hinton grew up enjoying reading. As she matured, she found that most of the books written for her age group held little interest for her. At fifteen, she began writing what would become her first published novel and during her junior year of high school completed *The Outsiders*. She has often been quoted as saying that she wrote the book so that she would "have something to read." Narrated by a character called Ponyboy—the outsider of the title—this book tells a tale of teenage social prejudice and gang violence. It was published when Hinton was a freshman at the University of Tulsa.

Struck with writer's block afterward, Hinton did not complete her second novel, *That Was Then, This Is Now*, until after she had graduated from college with a degree in education. While she was a student, she met her future husband, David Inhofe, who helped her break out of her writer's block by insisting that she write two pages a day before going out in the evening. Narrated by another tough out-

TITLES

The Outsiders, 1967

That Was Then, This Is Now, 1971

Rumble Fish, 1975

Tex, 1979

Taming the Star Runner, 1988

Hawkes Harbor, 2004

 p.338

sider, her second novel involves two boys who become as close as brothers, showing how drugs destroy the loyalty they feel for each other.

Hinton's next novel, *Rumble Fish* is again narrated by an outsider and continues with the familiar themes of absent parents, gang rumbles, violence, and death. *Taming the Star Runner* continues these themes but does not use an outsider as its narrator. Using the anonymous writer's point of view, it tells the story of a young boy who is sent away from the drugs, gangs, and violence of the city to live on his uncle's horse ranch in the country. Here Hinton draws on her love of horses and her experience as a published teenage writer.

Hinton was one of the first writers to create realistic characters in stories that speak to young adults in their own voices about topics that concern them. Her books are novels that young adults read and discuss among themselves. In 1988 the Young Adult Division of the American Library Association and the magazine *School Library Journal* awarded Hinton its first Margaret A. Edwards Award for authors whose books are "accepted by

 p.45

p.1

p.33

The Outsiders, the Movie

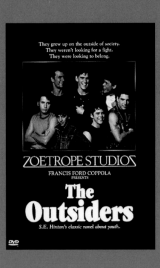

Hollywood has been kind to Hinton, filming four of her novels in reasonably good adaptations. *The Outsiders* (1983) was directed by Francis Ford Coppola and starred Matt Dillon. Dillon had appeared in the film version of *Tex* the previous year, and Hinton had taught him how to ride her horse, who appears in the film. Hinton acted as a consultant on the film and made a cameo appearance as a nurse. Most notable was the casting of young actors who went on to larger careers, including Emilio Estevez, Rob Lowe, C. Thomas Howell, Ralph Macchio, Patrick Swayze, and most notably Tom Cruise.

young people as an authentic voice that continues to illuminate their experiences and emotions, giving insight into their lives."

Four of S. E. Hinton's novels have been made into popular films. She also is the author of books for children. Despite her success, Hinton enjoys a private life. She does not enjoy traveling or public speaking and has stopped making public appearances.

– Ken Burles

Will Hobbs

Born: August 22, 1947; Pittsburgh, Pennsylvania

www.willhobbsauthor.com

Will Hobbs's love of nature and the outdoors is evident in all his novels. He has traveled through Alaska, the Grand Canyon, the Sierra Nevada, and isolated areas of the southwestern United States—all wilderness regions that have served as settings for his action-packed adventure novels. These remote locations provide his adolescent male **protagonists** with worthy venues for introspective reflection.

p.23

For seventeen years, William Carl Hobbs was known as "Mr. Hobbs" to the many junior high and high school students to whom he taught reading and English. He did not start writing until he was nearly forty. Although he wrote *Bearstone* first, *Changes in Latitude* (the title comes from a Jimmy Buffett song) was his first published book. *Bearstone* is the story of Cloyd, a Ute boy, who rediscovers his Native American heritage and the meaning of friendship with the help of an elderly rancher. The eight years and six complete rewritings that Hobbs invested in *Bearstone* started his journey as a full-time writer. He later continued Cloyd's story in *Beardance*.

Many of Hobbs's novels start from single images or experiences. A photograph of sea turtles launched *Changes in Latitude*. That picture led Hobbs to tell the story of two endangered species: the sea turtles and the disintegrating family of a boy named Travis.

Hobbs's next novel, *Downriver*, and its sequel, *River Thunder*, find Jesse and her companions tested by the Colorado River as it flows through the Grand Canyon, a locale well known to Hobbs, who has rowed down the canyon's wild river many times. However, some of his other novels required him to do original research. To write *The Big Wander*, he studied old books, maps, and television Westerns to bring alive the story of Clay's exploration of the region to be later flooded by Lake Powell during the early 1960's.

p.341

Hobbs departed from realism in *Kokopelli's Flute*, which blends fantasy with fact. Tepary Jones falls under an ancient spell that transforms him into a bushy-tailed wood rat at night. However, he is able to foil pothunters trying to loot ancient Anasazi ru-

342

Colorado River Crisis

A drought which began in 1999 caused the water levels in the reservoirs at both ends of the Grand Canyon to drop to nearly half of their capacity by 2004. The water from the Colorado River supplies some twenty-five million people in seven states, and more in Mexico. Should the drought continue, the Interior Department will have to restrict the amount of water taken out of the river within two to three years. Lake Powell, at the upper end of the Grand Canyon, was at 42% of capacity in 2004, the lowest since it was filled in 1970. Lake Mead, formed by Hoover Dam on the lower end, was at 59% capacity. The states relying on the river for water and electricity need to cooperate to avoid a serious, even disastrous, problem.

p.

ins and also saves his mother from a deadly disease. In another break from his usual coming-of-age adventure story, Hobbs wrote *Ghost Canoe*, which won the **Edgar Allan Poe Award** for Best Young Adult Mystery. In that story, a puzzling shipwreck that occurred in 1874 leads Nathan MacAllister, a lighthouse keeper's son, to suspect that someone survived the wreck. With the help of a local fisherman, Nathan uncovers the truth and discovers clues to a lost treasure.

Will Hobbs's command of sensory description allows his readers to step into the shoes of his characters. For this reason, many of his books have won awards from many national and state organizations. He is also the author of several picture books. Hobbs often appears at state and national professional conferences speaking about his novels.

– Kay Moore

Anasazi

The name Anasazi comes from the Navajo term meaning "the ancient ones" and applies to a group of ancient native people who lived in the American Southwest. We know of them from the architectural ruins scattered throughout New Mexico, Arizona, Utah, and Colorado. They built large villages of multistoried buildings constructed of cut sandstone. These ruins can be seen today at Chaco Canyon in New Mexico and Mesa Verde in Colorado. Sometime after 1400, the Anasazi abandoned these villages. Their descendants are the Pueblo Indians of the American Southwest.

Isabelle Holland

Born: June 16, 1920; Basel, Switzerland
Died: February 9, 2002; New York, New York

www.lib.usm.edu/%7Edegrum/html/research/
findaids/holland.htm

Isabelle Holland enjoyed a long and productive career as a writer of both young adult fiction and **gothic** mystery novels. Her young adult books are known for their fearless and frank treatment of such sensitive subjects as obesity, **homosexuality**, rape, and death. They are realistic and sensitive treatments of the need for acceptance of teenagers who are "different" or criticized by friends and family members. In *Dinah and the Green Fat Kingdom*, for example, an overweight girl is hounded by her older brother, cousin, and mother. In attaining the respect she deserves from others, Dinah serves as a model to other young people who face similar difficulties.

The daughter of an American diplomat, Holland was born in Switzerland and spent her early years in Guatemala and England. She did not live in the United States until 1940, after World War II began in Europe. She began writing in childhood and worked in publishing, mostly in **publicity**, until 1969, when she became a full-time writer. She sometimes wrote under the pen name Francesca Hunt.

Holland repeatedly examined the relationships between young people and adults, hoping to illuminate how adult actions or attitudes can shape young people's concepts of themselves. For example, her first novel, *Cecily*, probes the interactions between an awkward and unhappy teenager and her teacher at a prestigious English **boarding school**.

Holland's best-known book, *The Man Without a Face*, is about fourteen-year-old Charles Norstadt, a lonely and unloved boy who forms a friendship with

560
p.57
p.344
p.168

TITLES

Publicity

People employed in publicity in the publishing industry work to get attention for authors and the books that companies publish. Publicists work with newspapers and magazines to get the books reviewed. They schedule book-signing tours for the authors at bookstores and conventions across the country. They set up interviews in newspapers, magazines, radio, and television so authors can promote their books.

a teacher named Justin McLeod. Although horribly disfigured by facial scars, reclusive, and apparently homosexual, McLeod agrees to tutor Charles for his entrance exams to a private school. To Charles, McLeod becomes the friend and father he never had. Charles eventually finds that he can communicate with McLeod without words. From McLeod, Charles learns about trust and the many forms love can take. The book, which formed the basis for a 1993 film p.34 starring Mel Gibson, was listed among the American Library Association's **Best of the Best Books** for 1970-1983.

p.45

Of Love and Death and Other Journeys is often praised as Holland's best book. It follows fifteen-year-old Meg as she works through the loneliness and grief of her mother's cancer and eventual death. Through her struggle, Meg learns the value of life, love, and forgiveness. The book was a finalist for the National Book Award in 1976.

p.122

Isabelle Holland's characters are deep and fully developed. Readers can easily identify with them and feel compassion for them. She is an outstanding storyteller, and her grasp of human motivations is rarely off target. Her use of language is stylish, often lyrical. Her first-person narratives allow readers to discover for themselves the strengths and weaknesses of their often isolated characters and to probe the difficult family and social situations they face. Holland never retired from writing and continued working until her death in 2002.

– Faith Hickman Brynie

The Man Without a Face, the Movie

Isabelle Holland's novel was brought to the screen in 1993 by actor Mel Gibson in his debut as a director. This is one case where the movie adaptation differed substantially from the book and sparked a strong debate among fans of the book and fans of the movie. Gibson altered the sexual orientation of the main character which changes one aspect of his relationship with Charles. He also changed the ending. Read the book then see the movie. What do you think about the changes?

Dorothy Hoobler

Born: 1941; Philadelphia, Pennsylvania

A fourteen-year-old boy named Seikei is the central character in two historical mysteries by **Dorothy Hoobler** and her husband Thomas Hoobler, who have coauthored many books about young people meeting the challenges of the times in which they live. These mysteries have an interesting setting—eighteenth century Japan—and an appealing hero, who dreams of becoming a samurai warrior and willingly risks his life in the pursuit of honor and justice.

p.1

p.34

Dorothy Hoobler was born in Philadelphia, Pennsylvania, in 1941. She received her bachelor's degree from Wells College in 1963 and her master's degree from New York University in 1971. That same year she married Thomas Hoobler, who shares her interests in history, photography, gardening, music, and travel. Both of the Hooblers worked as editors. In 1973, however, Dorothy began devoting all her time to writing. Three years later, her husband left his other job to become a full-time writer. They had already brought out their first joint publication, *Frontier Diary* (1974). Other nonfiction works followed, most of them for young people. They included biographies such as *Margaret Mead: A Life in Science* (1974), historical books such as *The Voyages of Captain Cook* (1983), a series featuring "portraits" of people of various nationalities, and the American Family Album series, which dealt with various ethnic groups within the United States.

In 1991 Dorothy and Thomas Hoobler ventured into children's historical fiction, publishing the first

Samurai

Samurai were members of the Japanese military class. While they had a wide range of weapons available, their symbol was the sword. They lived according to a strict ethical code of *bushido* or the way of the warrior. It emphasized loyalty to one's master, self-discipline, respect, and ethical behavior. The *shogun* was the highest military officer. During Japanese history the role of the samurai changed from hired warrior, to government military man, to castle town warrior. After a long period of peace in Japan, the samurai was abolished in 1868.

volume in the Her Story series. The Century Kids books, novels about children living in different decades of the twentieth century, began appearing in 2000.

For their first historical mystery, *The Ghost in the Tokaido Inn*, these prolific writers drew on their long-standing interest in the Far East. This novel begins as a ghost story. A jewel is stolen from a samurai staying at an inn, and Seikei is certain that he saw a ghost commit the theft. However, a young girl, who is also a guest at the inn, is accused of taking the jewel. A crime-solving judge asks Seikei to help him investigate. Although his efforts put him in grave danger, Seikei persists, solves the mystery, and clears the girl.

In *The Demon in the Teahouse*, Seikei is again asked to gather information for the judge. Someone is murdering **geisha** girls, and there are also fires being set nearby. Seikei begins his investigation by taking a job at a teahouse. Soon he finds himself falsely accused of arson and realizes that again his detective work has put his own life at risk. In the end, Seikei discovers the truth, thus again proving his worth and perhaps moving him one step closer

Geisha

Geisha are Japanese women who act as professional hostesses. They go through a five to six year apprenticeship during which time they are known as *maiko*. They are taught traditional Japanese arts, including playing instruments, singing, dancing, flower arranging, calligraphy, the tea cere-

mony, conversation, and social skills. Geisha also learn how to dress in the traditional kimono and how to apply pale make-up and create traditional hair styles. The appearance of a geisha is unlike that of a contemporary Japanese woman. A geisha cannot marry. Because of the long apprenticeship and strict rules, the number of geisha is decreasing in modern Japan.

to realizing his dream of becoming a samurai.

Dorothy Hoobler has said that historical books help young people develop the understanding of other cultures which is so important if the world is to live in peace. Reviewers agree that not only are the mysteries that Hoobler and her husband have coauthored exciting and suspenseful, but they also offer valuable insights into Japanese culture.

— Rosemary M. Canfield Reisman

Monica Hughes

Born: November 3, 1925; Liverpool, England

www.ecn.ab.ca/mhughes/index.html

Monica Hughes came to writing relatively late in her life but rapidly made up for lost time by cleverly combining many elements of her remarkably various biography in her thoughtful speculative fiction. The daughter of a noted mathematician, E. L. Ince, Hughes was educated at a **convent** in Harrogate in northern England and at Edinburgh University before serving in the **Women's Royal Naval Service** during World War II. She then worked as a dress designer and emigrated to Canada in 1952. There she worked as a laboratory technician in Ottawa until her marriage in 1957.

Hughes's first novel, *Gold Fever Trail*, was followed by further explorations of Canadian colonial history and race relations. Other books include *The Ghost Dance Caper, The Treasure of the Long Sault* and *Log Jam*. She often extrapolates similar themes in the science fiction for which she is best known. *Crisis on Conshelf Ten* and its sequel *Earthdark*, for example, compare and contrast colonial societies restricted in different ways, while *Beyond the Dark River* and *Ring-Rise, Ring-Set* examine Native American cultures in futuristic settings.

Crises of adolescence are modeled in many different ways in Hughes's work. Her most successful early works, the books in her Isis trilogy, offer painstaking accounts of their heroine's attempts to come to terms with her chimerical identity. *Hunter in the Dark* is a naturalistic account of self-confrontation. The challenging circumstances in which such characters operate are further exaggerated in *The Tomor-*

TITLES

row City, whose heroine is adrift in a society that has been brainwashed into conformity by a well-intentioned but over-zealous computer, and in two pairs of novels set in similarly grim futures, one consisting of *Devil on My Back* and *The Dream Catcher*, the other of *Sandwriter* and *The Promise*. The subtly horrific *Invitation to the Game*, in which a future society attempts to secure its Utopian ambitions by exporting its troublesome adolescents, is a further addition to this group. This theme is revisited, set against an even darker background, in *The Other Place*.

The Crystal Drop is an environmentalist **fantasy** set in a drought-stricken near future. *A Handful of Seeds*, written in behalf of UNICEF Canada as a protest against the plight of street children all over the world, is about a displaced child who carries chili, corn, and bean seeds into a city ghetto and plants a garden amid the rubble. The young hero of *The Golden Aquarians* realizes that the terra-forming project in which his father is involved will result in the genocide of the meek amphibious creatures that are native to the planet.

p.8

Women's Royal Naval Service (WRNS)

The Women's Royal Naval Service was created in 1917 during World War I. Women were recruited to serve on shore as cooks, clerks, telegraph operators, electricians, and code specialists so more men could go to sea. At the end of the war in 1918, some 6,000 women were serving in WRNS. The service ended with the end of the war, but it was restarted in 1939 during World War II. By 1944, some 74,000 women served in WRNS. In 1977, it became regulated by the Naval Discipline Act, and in 1993 it was integrated into the Royal Navy. Today women serve in the Royal Navy and have equal access to jobs and working conditions on shore and aboard ships.

Governor General's Literary Award

The first Governor General's Literary Awards were made in 1937. Today, they are the most prestigious literary awards in Canada. The awards originally were administered by the Canadian Authors Association. In 1959, the Canada Council took over the awards and added prizes for works written in French (one of Canada's provinces, Quebec, is French-speaking). The Council integrated the Canada Council Prizes for Children's Literature and Translation into the Governor General's Literary Awards in 1987. Since 1951, the award has included a cash prize. The amount of the prize has been $15,000 since 2000.

Hughes branched out into dark fantasy in *Where Have You Been, Billy Boy?*, which features a time machine disguised as a carousel. *Castle Tourmandyne* features a sinister Victorian dollhouse. In *The Seven Magpies*, pupils at the "safe school" to which the heroine is evacuated in World War II tamper with ancient magic. In *The Faces of Fear* a wheelchair-bound girl's escape into virtual reality proves unexpectedly hazardous. The protagonist in *The Story Box* must broaden his imaginative horizons when a storyteller is shipwrecked on his native island, where fiction is banned and dreams are suppressed. This book marked a return to the earnest and heartfelt moralistic fantasy which is Hughes's strength.

 p.233

Monica Hughes's writing honors include Canada's Governor General's Literary Award for Children's Literature for *The Guardian of Isis* and *Hunter in the Dark*. The latter also won a Canadian Library Association **Young Adult Book Award**.

— Brian Stableford

Mollie Hunter

Born: June 30, 1922; Longniddry, East Lothian, Scotland

http://www.lib.usm.edu/%7Edegrum/findaids/hunter.htm

Mollie Hunter has published more than twenty novels, as well as short stories, plays, screenplays, articles on Scottish history, and an acclaimed book on writing for children. She has also written historical fiction, picture books, and fantasies for much younger readers. Her fantasies are filled with Celtic lore and mischievous ancient spirits doing battle with the modern dispassionate "spirits" of technology. p.1

Born Maureen Mollie Hunter McVeigh, Hunter grew up in Scotland listening to her mother's and great-grandmother's stories of the Scottish past and she longed to study their original sources. However, her father's death left the family in such poverty that Mollie had to leave school at the age of fourteen to work in an Edinburgh flower shop owned by relatives. Determined to further her education, she took night classes while she worked in Edinburgh and did research at the National Library of Scotland. p.353 She learned Scottish history and Celtic lore by studying old documents and texts. While still a teenager, she married Michael McIlwaithe. As her sons grew up, she invented stories for them, and these stories led to her first book in the early 1950's.

Hunter's young adult novels fall into two broad categories: historical fiction and contemporary realism. Two of her best-known historical novels feature adolescent boys coming to the aid of famous Scottish monarchs. In *You Never Knew Her as I Did*, seventeen-year-old Will Page sets out to rescue Mary, Queen of Scots, from prison, and his ingenious idea for freeing her results in a thrilling escape story. In another story of ingenuity and daring, sixteen-year-old Martin Crawford lands a job as courier for the fourteenth century Scottish king Robert the Bruce in *The King's Swift Rider*. Hunter's well-researched and realistic novel about the famous rebellion to restore Robert to the Scottish throne is marked by high adventure, espionage, heroism, bloodshed, and tragedy.

Independent-minded young girls people Hunter's contemporary realism. *Cat, Herself* is a coming-of-age story of Catriona (Cat) McPhie, the scrappy, strong-willed daughter of traveling **tinkers** who are p.354 ridiculed and harassed by villagers wherever they set up camp. Cat rebels against both the ridicule her people endure from outsiders and the rigid gender roles within her own community. When her father offers to teach her a man's skills, Cat worries about teasing, but accepts his offer. The novel is both deeply psychological and highly adventurous, with several life-and-death episodes that demand Cat's courage and ultimately lead her through anger,

National Library of Scotland

The National Library of Scotland has its roots in the Library of the Faculty of Advocates. It was founded in 1689 and given the legal right to own one copy of every published book in Britain. In the 1920's the collection was given to the nation and, in 1925, the National Library of Scotland was dedicated. Since that time, it has become an international research institution and the world center for the study of Scotland and the Scots. Built on George IV Bridge in Edinburgh, the library is a popular site for people researching their family tree. The library mounts special exhibitions showcasing the permanent collections.

grief, and acceptance. A sequel to Hunter's autobiographical novel *A Sound of Chariots* (1972), *Hold on to Love* tells the story of another fiercely independent fifteen-year-old girl, Bridie McShane, who overcomes immense obstacles to make her way as a writer—and in the process, finds love.

Mollie Hunter was awarded the British Library Association's 1974 **Carnegie Medal**, given to an outstanding children's book, for *The Stronghold*; her novels *You Never Knew Her as I Did* and *Cat, Herself* earned major library awards. A number of her books have been serialized on **BBC**-Radio.

p.4

p.6

– Jan Allister

Tinker

A tinker was a person who traveled from place to place and made a living mending pots and pans. Tinkers were of low social standing and were treated similar to gypsys. In our modern world, where we can easily buy and replace worn out household wares, it is difficult to imagine someone repairing a hole in a pot.

Henry James

Born: April 15, 1843; New York, New York
Died: February 28, 1916; London, England

www.kirjasto.sci.fi/hjames.htm

Although **Henry James**'s writing is considered dated and somewhat difficult to read by many modern readers, two of his novels, *Daisy Miller* and *The Turn of the Screw*, frequently appear on supplementary reading lists in secondary schools.

Born into an affluent, intellectual family in New York, James spent much of his childhood in Europe, particularly England, France, and Switzerland, and was educated in private schools and by tutors. He entered Harvard Law School in 1862 but spent most of his time at Harvard attending lectures on literature. In Cambridge and later as he traveled independently throughout Europe, he met the most notable writers and intellectuals of his day. Eventually, he settled permanently in England and became a British subject.

Daisy Miller deals, as many of James's novels do, with social stratification. Daisy is the daughter of *nouveau riche* parents and is traveling in Europe with her permissive mother and spoiled younger brother, Randolph. In Vevey, Switzerland, the beautiful Daisy attracts the attention of Frederick Winterbourne, a well-born American expatriate of independent means. Winterbourne's aunt, Mrs. Costello, refuses to meet

p.5

356

TITLES

Daisy Miller, 1879

The Turn of the Screw, 1898

Nouveau riche

This French term that has been adopted into English means one who recently has become rich. In a society with a class structure, it suggests that the newly rich are not as socially acceptable as those who have been rich for generations. In Henry James's fictional Europe, Americans are suspicious because of their recent wealth. Even in American society today, the term *nouveau riche* describes someone with little taste or manners. Many of these newly rich Americans make their money on Wall Street, symbolized by the sculpture of the bull.

Daisy, whom she considers common. Winterbourne's attraction to Daisy becomes a problem and then wanes when Daisy goes to Rome and becomes involved with Sr. Giovanelli, a lusty Italian who pursues her. Winterbourne shuns Daisy, acknowledging his aunt's judgment that she is his social inferior. Late one night, Winterbourne encounters Daisy and Giovanelli in the Coliseum, a hazardous place to be because of the danger of ma-laria. Winterbourne is shocked to find Daisy there, but Giovanelli explains that Daisy wanted to see the Coliseum by moonlight so he has complied. Shortly afterward Daisy falls ill with malaria. A week later, she dies, but not before she has sent Winterbourne a note telling him that she was never engaged to Giovanelli, as Winterbourne had assumed. Giovanelli has also confirmed that he and Daisy would never marry. Standing beside her grave in Rome's American cemetery, Winterbourne finally realizes that Daisy is at heart an innocent and that he has been in love with her all along. James emphasizes in this novella the perils of innocence.

The Turn of the Screw is one of a handful of mystery stories that most critics consider a literary mas-

p.357

p.96

terpiece. The story is based on the diary of an unnamed **governess**. She is charged with looking after a brother and sister, Miles and Flora, after the death of their former governess, Miss Jessel. Miss Jessel's lover was Peter Quint, the deceased valet of the children's uncle. Both Miss Jessel and Quint appear to the governess, but only she can see them. At first, she refrains from mentioning their ghostly appearances to the children but, terrorized by their images, she eventually admits seeing them. At that point, Miles collapses and dies of no apparent cause in the governess's arms.

The Turn of the Screw is a study in ambiguity. As it unfolds, it raises more questions than it answers. Are the ghosts the product of the governess's imagination or do they actually exist? The story's principals are of the same social class—the moneyed aristocracy—that populate most of James's novels.

– R. Baird Shuman

Malaria

Malaria is a serious infection carried by mosquitos in tropical and subtropical regions. It causes recurring bouts of severe fever, chills, sweating, vomiting, and damage to the kidneys, blood, brain, and liver. The ancient Greeks and Romans had tried to control malaria by draining swamps and marshes but met with little success. During the construction of the Panama Canal (1904-1914), General William Gorgas directed a program to drains swamps, apply chemicals to the land, and treat workers with quinine. Malaria was eliminated in the Canal Zone in 1910. In the 1940's and 1950's, the insecticide DDT was sprayed widely to kill the mosquitoes. By the mid-1960's, malaria was controlled in North America and Europe. Since then, there has been little success controlling malaria in other parts of the world, but many international organizations continue to work on the prevention and control of this disease.

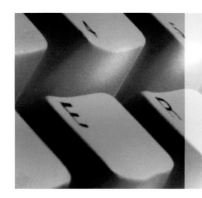

Francisco Jimenez

Born: June 29, 1943; San Pedro, Thlaquepaque, Mexico

Francisco Jimenez uses the immediacy and authenticity of the first-person point of view to relate his own family's journey from a small village near Guadalajara, Mexico, to the United States and their experiences in their adopted country. Realistically and vividly, his books portray the injustice, poverty, and impermanence **migrant workers** p.67 face. Jimenez conveys these themes in simple, yet poetically metaphorical language. Fully realized without being sentimental, his characters are warm and loving, but are also sometimes angry and bitter. Family and its members love for one another is the sustaining force in Jimenez's works.

The Circuit is a collection of short autobiographical stories told in sequential order. Its stories chronicle the first fourteen years of a character based on Jimenez himself, Panchito, and his family. Jimenez's second book, *Breaking Through*, depicts Panchito's teenage years after he and his family are caught p.359 by U.S. immigration officers and forced to leave their home in California. Although the stories skip over several time periods, they are unified by their themes and Panchito's emotional and physical development.

Francisco Jimenez and his family left Mexico in search of a better life and to find the American Dream. To survive, they took the typical jobs avail- p.360 able to **migrant farmworkers** and thus entered an endless cycle—a physical and symbolic "circuit"—of poverty, temporary homes, and backbreaking labor as they followed harvests from county to county, ac-

U.S. Citizenship and Immigration Services

This agency, formerly know as the INS (Immigration and Naturalization Service), is responsible for processing citizenship, green card, visa, and other types of applications for permission to live and work in the U.S. Its agents also patrol the borders and attempt to catch those who do not have permission to enter or live in the United States. The agency is a part of the Department of Homeland Security. Since the attacks on the World Trade Center on September 11, 2001, the responsibility for guarding the borders also includes keeping out suspected terrorists.

cepting low wages wherever they could find them.

The Circuit realistically chronicles Jimenez's own family's journey and the impact that the endless cycle of poverty has on the hopes and aspirations of its stories' central characters. The migrant workers are forced to live in tents, garages, or dilapidated houses with neither electricity nor indoor plumbing. Unless the workers are lucky enough to find scraps of linoleum in the garbage dump, they usually live on dirt floors and fill gaps in the walls with old newspapers to keep rats and snakes from entering.

Jimenez's fictional Panchito—as Jimenez himself once did—finds brief respites from the physical poverty when he attends school, which has heating and electric lights. However, because he cannot start school until the harvests are finished in mid-November and cannot speak English, he often faces prejudice and discrimination. With tenacity and hard work, Panchito breaks through the language barrier and dreams of staying in one place long enough to make friends, attend school on a regular basis, and have a place to call home.

FRANCISCO JIMENEZ

César Chávez

César Chávez was a Mexican American whose family worked as migrant farmworkers in California. He experienced the horrible conditions under which these workers lived. In the 1950's, he began to work to improve those conditions. Chávez formed the Farm Workers Association to organize migrant workers. The union, renamed the National Farm Workers Association, went on strike. A grape boycott followed that lasted from 1965 to 1970. The labor movement in the U.S. was influenced by Chávez and his nonviolent methods. The state of California has established a special holiday in honor of the labor leader.

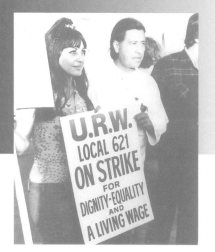

The sequel to *The Circuit, Breaking Through*, focuses on Jimenez's high school years. Panchito has now lost his innocence and learns to be successful. Jimenez realistically portrays the clash of cultures in this sequel as Panchito becomes more accustomed to American ideas: the importance of wearing the right clothes, having the right friends, and beginning to challenge his father's demand for unquestioning loyalty and respect. His family cannot support him financially, so he works at odd jobs before and after school. His friends cannot give him much moral support because they cannot understand his longings. Panchito's intense desire to succeed enables him to persevere against these obstacles and provides all readers with hope.

Francisco Jimenez's *The Circuit* and *Breaking Through* were honored with American Library Association Best Books for Young Adults awards.

– Sharon K. Wilson

p.4

p.48

Diana Wynne Jones

Born: August 16, 1934; London, England

http://www.harpercollins.co.uk/authors/
default.asp?id=2989

p.87

362

Diana Wynne Jones published an adult novel and a novel for younger children before writing young adult **fantasy**. She draws wildly different ideas into combinations never before attempted, often with remarkable effect. She introduces fantastic materials into contemporary scenarios in a matter-of-fact way that resembles the methods of **Magical Realist** writers. However, she does this in a way that favors the magical elements over the realistic ones, creating conclusions that are sometimes so far-reaching as to be casually decisive.

After some early experiments with comedy, most notably in *Eight Days of Luke* and Secondary World fantasies of the Dalemark series—consisting of *Cart and Cwidder*, *Drowned Ammet*, *The Spellcoats* and *The Crown of Dalemark*—Jones began to perfect her unconventional narrative method in the Chrestomanci series, featuring a troubleshooting wizard who assists various adolescents to come to terms with growing magical powers: *Charmed Life*, *The Magicians of Caprona*, *Witch Week* and *The Lives of Christopher Chant*.

The alternative worlds featured in the Chrestomanci series are further elaborated in *The Homeward Bounders*, whose young hero is cast adrift in worlds used as gaming arenas by godlike beings. After meeting other wanderers who have meekly adapted to their fate, he becomes a rebel leader. Similar time- and space-twisting premises give rise to the suspenseful identity-searching plots of *The Time of the Ghost* and *Fire and Hemlock*, the remarkable

TITLES

The Ogre Downstairs, 1974

Cart and Cwidder, 1975

Dogsbody, 1975

Eight Days of Luke, 1975

Power of Three, 1976

Charmed Life, 1977

Drowned Ammet, 1977

The Spellcoats, 1979

The Magicians of Caprona, 1980

The Homeward Bounders, 1981

The Time of the Ghost, 1981

Witch Week, 1982

Archer's Goon, 1984

Fire and Hemlock, 1984

The Skivers' Guide, 1984

Warlock at the Wheel and Other Stories, 1984

Howl's Moving Castle, 1986

A Tale of Time City, 1987

The Lives of Christopher Chant, 1988

Castle in the Air, 1990

Aunt Maria, 1991 (publ. in England as *Black Maria*)

intricacies of *Archer's Goon*, *A Tale of Time City* and *Hexwood*, and the flamboyant comedy of *Howl's Moving Castle* and its sequel *Castle in the Air*. *Aunt Maria* is a comedy in a subtler and more ironic vein, as is *Wild Robert*, whose charming like-named ghost is horrified by the state of the modern world. The **protagonist** of *Deep Secret*, who has the taxing responsibility of making sure that his civilization does not collapse, experiences a similar sad distress.

p.23

Jones's impatience with the cliches of contemporary genre fantasy led her to the **parody** *Tough Guide to Fantasyland*, whose spirit was further extended in the broad comedy of *Dark Lord of Derkholm* and its sequel *Year of the Griffin*. These comedies are delightfully playful.

p.36

Although Jones's ornate literary method occasionally leaves clusters of loose ends, its use has allowed her to build up a strikingly original body of work. Her shorter fiction tends to spill out of the young adult category on one side or the other, but *Everard's Ride* collects two fine novellas which are more mature than the three in *Stopping for a Spell* (1989) while not being as elaborate as the majority of

Magical Realism

Magical Realism was introduced into literary criticism during the mid-1960's and early 1970's with the translation of works by Latin American writers such as Gabriel García Márquez and Jorge Amado. In their novels, they freely mixed common everyday experience with supernatural situations. The supernatural was treated as real and normal. This encouraged other writers, especially in the field of fantasy, to include folklore from cultures other than the white European tradition into their writing.

the items in *A Sudden Wild Magic* (1992). Her best novels—particularly *The Homeward Bounders* and *Archer's Goon*—have the rare distinction of being unlike anything done before or since, and constitute authentic literary treasures.

Diana Wynne Jones's writing honors include **Boston Globe-Horn Honor Book** awards for both *Archer's Goon* and *Howl's Moving Castle*.

– Brian Stableford

Gene Kemp

Born: December 27, 1926; Wigginton, Staffordshire, England

Born Gene Rushton, **Gene Kemp** grew up in Tamworth in the north Midlands of England. Her earliest publications were stories for younger children featuring a famous local breed of pigs. After studying at Exeter University she settled in Devon and worked as a teacher during the 1960's and 1970's. Her first novel, set in Cricklepit Combined School, was *The Turbulent Term of Tyke Tiler*. It was an immediate success; it won a **Carnegie Medal** and quickly became established in British school curricula as a remedy to sexist thinking. p.

Kemp's second novel set at Cricklepit, *Gowie Corby Plays Chicken*, revealed what was to become a long preoccupation with dubious hauntings. However, her most successful ghost stories are those with settings carefully designed to fit them. Her work in this vein extends from *The Clock Tower Ghost*, a comedy set firmly in the tradition of Oscar Wilde's **"The Canterville Ghost,"** to *The Hairy Hands*, a suspenseful tale based on a Dartmoor legend. *Jason Bodger and the Priory Ghost* is a comic history lesson that is neither as funny nor as informative as it attempts to be, but *Bluebeard's Castle* is far more successful. The eldest of four sisters from a poor family marries a millionaire movie-maker. However, the sister's fairy-tale transformation falls apart when she and her sisters discover something nasty in the dungeons of a castle in the millionaire's Wonderland theme park. *Snaggletooth's Mystery* re- p.36

turns to the dark underside of Cricklepit Combined School; an excavation of the school's foundations exposes an unexpected link to children of another era, who had to contend with a cholera epidemic.

Kemp's naturalistic accounts of the agony of young underachievers, of which the best is *Just Ferret*, are worthy attempts to attract sympathy to a neglected sector of the school population. This type of work is elaborated in her novels featuring slightly older **protagonists**. For example, the hapless protagonist of *No Place Like* is a magnet for trouble that he is unable to handle until he is finally forced to begin the **Herculean** task of coming to terms with himself and his circumstances. The title character of *Juniper* has problems when her father leaves home, which are compounded when she is stalked. The protagonist of *I Can't Stand Losing* has to come to grips with the fact that losing is something that no one outside of a comic book can hope to avoid indefinitely.

Most of Gene Kemp's novels are thin on plot— none more so than *The Well*'s real life collection of anecdotes about growing up in a village cloned from Tamworth. However, the best of her books make up for their lack of structure with a low key moral message and a spirit of goodwill. Kemp never managed to repeat the success of *The Turbulent Term of Tyke*

"The Canterville Ghost"

Oscar Wilde's short story "The Canterville Ghost" was first published in 1887. It is a comical story about an American family who purchases a haunted English manor house. The Americans, however, do not believe in ghosts. Wilde used the story to comically contrast the crude *nouveau riche* Americans against the upper class British. The story continues to be popular with young readers and has been made into movies for both cinema and television.

Tyler. However, as with many of her characters, her underachievement is only superficial. Her best work champions the underdogs and outsiders, and its humor is supported by a welcome generosity of spirit.

– Brian Stableford

Herculean

Herculean means something is of extraordinary power or strength. It comes from "Hercules," the most famous hero of Greek mythology. Hercules was the son of Zeus, the most powerful of the Greek gods. He was born with great strength and showed great courage throughout his life. For his courage, he went to live with the gods on Mount Olympus. Hercules appears in many Greek stories, and his image adorns ancient artwork. Hercules' life has been the subject of many movies, and Disney even made an animated feature about him.

M. E. Kerr

Born: May 27, 1927; Auburn, New York

www.mekerr.com

M. E. Kerr's young adult books are uncompromising looks at the tougher issues that many teenagers face. Most of them are written from the point of view of male characters from the mid- to upper-teens. Her books address issues that go much deeper than typical adolescent angst, as her characters face problems such as various forms of prejudice, chemical addictions, ambiguous sexual identity, acquired immunodeficiency syndrome (AIDS), and the effects of war and the toll it takes on people at home. Moreover, the resolutions of Kerr's stories are neither easy nor simplistic; they are often ragged, much like the resolutions of problems in real life.

Born Marijane Agnes Meaker in 1927 in New York, Kerr became interested in books and writers at an early age. After finishing college she drifted into **freelance writing** for magazines and quickly made it her profession. She was fascinated by the idea of pen names and wrote under several, including Mary James, Ann Aldrich, and Vin Packer. Using those names, she did many types of writing, including mysteries and slice-of-life novels for adult readers. However, it was only after Kerr read Louise Fitzhugh's popular *Harriet the Spy* (1964) that she turned to writing young adult novels.

Kerr did not publish her first young adult novel, *Dinky Hocker Shoots Smack!*, until she was forty-five years old. This book contains misfit characters who meet when the young male narrator must find a new home for his cat and meets Dinky, an overweight girl who is trying to find acceptance. The

368►

500►

Freelance Writer

Freelance refers to someone who works independently and is not permanently associated with any one employer. A freelance writer, for example, accepts writing assignments from many different companies. These assignments can be to write articles for publication in magazines, to write news stories about the company called press releases, or to create newletters or other corporate publications. The term originally applied to a knight or soldier who could be hired by a military leader, a "lance for hire."

book deals with the most important relationships in teenagers' lives and how being different from the norm affects those relationships.

Kerr has also made the formerly taboo subject of teenage homosexuality and bisexuality a recurrent theme in her novels. *I'll Love You When You're More Like Me* and later books such as *Deliver Us from Evie* deal with issues that are associated with alternative lifestyles. Her novel *Night Kites* concerns teenagers infected by the AIDS virus.

M. E. Kerr has won numerous awards for her uncompromising portrayals of serious issues. Her most notable honors are a **Christopher Award** for *Gentle Hands* in 1979, a Golden Kite Award for *Little, Little*

p.57

p.369

p.11

in 1981, and the Margaret A. Edwards Award for Lifetime Achievement in 1993. In 1983 she told her own life story in *Me! Me! Me! Me! Me! Not a Novel*.

— Emma Harris

Alternative Lifestyle

An alternative lifestyle differs from what most people consider normal. Gay and lesbian lifestyles are often termed "alternative" because they do not involve a relationship between a man and a woman that leads to marriage and a family. However, as psychologists have come to recognize that "alternative" is not a negative but a different way in which some people find balance in life, the term has lost some of its negative meaning to society as a whole.

Stephen King

Born: September 21, 1947; Portland, Maine

www.stephenking.com

Stephen King has written more than fifty **best-selling** books. Many of his characters are young adults who confront both ordinary and extraordinary problems. Most of them succeed in overcoming those challenges, but some fail.

p.38

When King was two years old, his father deserted his family. Afterward, his mother moved him and his older brother around the country before finally settling in Durham, Maine, when King was eleven. Despite his unsettled family life, King started writing at the age of seven and began submitting stories to professional magazines when he was only twelve. He started his first novel while he was still in high school and finally made his first fiction sale at the age of twenty. Meanwhile, he studied English at the University of Maine, from which he graduated in 1970. There he met Tabitha Spruce, whom he married the following year and with whom he had three children. After graduation, he worked in a laundry and taught high-school English while continuing to write on the side.

King's first big success was the horror novel *Carrie*. After its publisher sold the paperback rights to that book, King quit teaching to concentrate on writing full time. For almost a year, he and his family lived in Colorado, which he used as the setting for *The Shining* and portions of *The Stand*. They then returned permanently to Maine, in which King has set many of his other books. Soon he was publishing books so frequently that his publishers feared he was saturating the market. He then created the

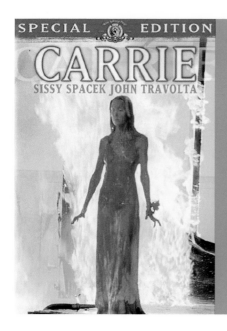

SPECIAL EDITION
CARRIE
SISSY SPACEK JOHN TRAVOLTA

Carrie, the Movie

In 1976, Brian De Palma directed the film version of King's first novel *Carrie*. The small budget film became a big success at the box office and introduced several future stars. Sissy Spacek, then in her twenties, starred as high-school student Carrie. Her performance brought the character to life and earned her an Academy Award nomination for best actress. John Travolta, who was appearing in a television series, made his big-screen debut in *Carrie*. He also went on to a highly successful career in the movies.

pseudonym Richard Bachman, under which he published a number of novels, such as *The Regulators*. He has also collaborated on novels with author Peter Straub.

Several of King's books are about young adult characters who are unpopular in high school. The title character of *Carrie* is a composite of two social misfits whom he knew when he was growing up but with an added peculiarity: **telekinetic** powers. The novel is a retelling of the Cinderella story: The unpopular Carrie is taken to her high school's prom by one of the most popular boys in the school and is crowned prom queen; then a vicious practical joke that a rich classmate plays on her triggers her telekinetic powers with disastrous results for everyone at the prom. In *Christine*, bullies harass high-school senior Arnie Cunningham until he acquires a magical 1958 Plymouth Fury, which he names "Christine." The car takes a terrible revenge on Arnie's enemies but then

p.306

The Accident

In June, 1999, Stephen King was walking along the road near his home in North Lovell, Maine. The driver of a van coming behind him lost control and hit King. King was seriously injured and was taken to the hospital, then helicoptered to a larger hospital. After surgeries and a long period of recovery, King struggled to begin writing again. In 2000, he published *On Writing: A Memoir of the Craft*. His first novel published after the accident was *Dreamcatcher* (2001). While there was speculation that King would retire after the accident, he continues to publish and to collaborate in television and other media.

turns on Arnie himself after he begins to date the prettiest girl in his school. In *The Stand* Harold Lauter is an ugly, overweight teenager when an artificial virus wipes out over 91 percent of the world's population.

Two of the four novellas collected in *Different Seasons* feature young adult characters. Todd Bowden in "Apt Pupil" is an athletic and attractive honor student who reveals his dark side when he discovers a Nazi war criminal secretly living in his neighborhood. All four of the main characters in "The Body" are twelve-year-old boys. One of them, Gordon Lachance, is King's most autobiographical character.

p.371
Many of Stephen King's books and stories have been adapted to **film** and television. King has also written original screenplays, and he directed *Maximum Overdrive* (1986), a film based on his short story "Trucks." He has even acted in a few movies. Because he is so popular and draws huge crowds, King rarely makes public appearances.

– Thomas R. Feller

Barbara Kingsolver

Born: April 8, 1955; Annapolis, Maryland

www.kingsolver.com/home/index.asp

Barbara Kingsolver's novels all center on three significant themes: the need for social justice and multicultural interaction, the importance of nature, and the role of family and community. All of these aspects are present in her own life as well. She also writes essays, nonfiction, and short stories.

Kingsolver was reared in rural Kentucky where she began writing at an early age. Her interest in science and her deep love of nature also led her to earn a biology degree from De Pauw University, where she became interested in many social causes. She later entered the University of Arizona to earn a master's degree in science but left to pursue her writing career. Between 1985 and 1987, she worked as a **freelance writer** and wrote her first novel, *The Bean Trees*, in her spare time.

The Bean Trees tells the story of Taylor Greer, a young girl from Kentucky who leaves her small hometown in search of adventure. Along the way, a Cherokee woman pushes an abused toddler into Taylor's car and asks Taylor to take care of her. Taylor names the infant Turtle because of her strong grip and drives west to Tucson where she meets many people who help her to raise

.368

TITLES

The Bean Trees, 1988

Pigs in Heaven, 1993

The Poisonwood Bible, 1998

the child. These friends also teach her the lesson of the book: like "the bean trees" (Turtle's name for **wisteria** vines) which depend on microscopic bugs to nourish their roots, people need friends around them to help them grow. Through Taylor, Turtle, and their friends, Kingsolver explores the issues of family, community, social justice, and nature.

p.3

Pigs in Heaven, Kingsolver's third novel, is the sequel to *The Bean Trees*. Turtle is now six and Taylor's right to adopt her is being challenged by Annawake Fourkiller, a Cherokee lawyer who believes that Turtle belongs with her biological family's community on the Cherokee reservation. In their battle for custody, Kingsolver also explores the roles that family, social justice, and culture play in shaping people's lives.

In contrast to Kingsolver's other novels, *The Poisonwood Bible* is set in Africa and focuses on a missionary family's problems adjusting to their new cultural environment. The novel is also interesting for its use of five different narrators. the mother and her four daughters each narrate a different chapter of the book and each has a different opinion about their new home. However, all of them eventually discover that community,

Wisteria

Wisteria, a legume or bean, is a very hardy vine that is popular in gardens. It has beautiful and fragrant cascading flowers that bloom in the spring, usually between April and June. The flowers can be purple, blue, pink, or white. There are Japanese, Chinese, American, and Kentucky wisteria, with the Japanese variety having the longest clusters of flowers. Wisteria can be trimmed to grow in many different ways. In most gardens the vine is trained to grow over an arbor so that the flowers hang from the supporting structure. They can also be trained to drape on the side of a building.

The Bellwether Prize for Fiction

Founded and funded by Barbara Kingsolver, the Bellwether Prize is awarded in even years to the author of an unpublished manuscript of "serious literary fiction that addresses issues of social justice and the impact of culture and politics on human relationships." The author must be a U.S. citizen who writes in English and has previously published but has not sold more than 10,000 copies of a book. The honored author receives a cash prize of $25,000 and is guaranteed publication of the manuscript by a major publisher.

nature and cultural tolerance are the keys to their survival.

Barbara Kingsolver has received many awards for her writing, including the **National Book Award of South Africa** for *The Poisonwood Bible* and the **National Humanities Medal**, the highest award for services in the arts in the United States. She was also a finalist for the **Pulitzer Prize** and the **PEN**/**Faulkner Award** (also for *The Poisonwood Bible*) and has established an award of her own called the **Bellwether Prize**, which is given to writers who create literature that promotes social change. Working on the theme of respect for other cultures and nature, Kingsolver is one of America's finest contemporary authors.

– Kristin Brunnemer

723

p.137

p.375

Annette Curtis Klause

Born: June 20, 1953; Bristol, England

eve7k.com/klause/author/index.php

Annette Curtis Klause writes horror stories and science fiction for young adults. Although her characters are not always humans, they always face human problems and dilemmas with the kind of gutsy courage that readers admire. For example, in *The Silver Kiss*, her first novel, Zoe's mother is dying, and Zoe needs a friend. She gets more than she bargains for, however, when Simon shows up at her door in the middle of the night. Simon is a **vampire** seeking revenge for the murder of his mother three centuries earlier. *The Silver Kiss* is both a love story and a suspense tale, charged with the energy of emergent sexuality and the enigmas of death and dying. p.30

Klause's second novel, *Alien Secrets*, is a mystery set in the future aboard a spacecraft. Expelled from school in disgrace, seventh-grader Puck travels to another planet to join her xenobiologist parents. On the spaceship, she meets an alien named Hush, a Shoowa recently liberated from enslavement by the villainous Grakks, whose evil is far from finished. A missing art object, some Shoowa ghosts, and smugglers and space cops round out this futuristic suspense tale.

Blood and Chocolate is the story of a sixteen-year-old **werewolf**, Vivian Gandillon. She and her pack have recently moved to the Maryland suburbs. Although Vivian has trouble fitting in among hu- p.377

mans, she falls in love with one. The human, whom the pack labels a "meat boy," is to Vivian as rich and smooth as chocolate. When a gruesome murder throws suspicion on the pack, the wolf people face detection, and Vivian must chose between being human and being animal. One reviewer pointed out that this novel can be read as feminist fiction, a smoldering romance, a rite-of-passage story, or even a piercing reflection on human nature. Another reviewer described its complex plot as "fueled by politics, insanity, intrigue, sex, blood lust, and adolescent longings, and driven by a set of vividly scary creatures to a blood-curdling climax."

p.87
Klause grew up hearing imaginative stories from her father. An avid reader of **fantasy**, horror, and science fiction early in her life, Klause has said she writes the books she would have enjoyed reading when she was young. At the age of fourteen, she read fantasy writer Jane Gaskell's *The Shiny Narrow Grin* (1964). That book inspired her to write a series p.303 of poems about **vampires**. Years later, those same poems provided the starting point for *The Silver Kiss*.

Klause's writing is crisp and lyrical, and her talents for language and characterization lend subtlety to plots that are unabashedly raw. The **American**

Werewolf

In folklore, a werewolf is an individual who becomes a wolf when the moon is full. He is only active at night and eats children and dead bodies. He can be killed by a silver arrow or a silver bullet. When he dies, he returns to his human form. The myth of the werewolf has existed in Western culture since the ancient Greeks. In the Middle Ages, the Church believed the wolf was evil personified and a servant of the Devil. When this belief went out of favor, the idea of the wolf as evil continued in people's minds.

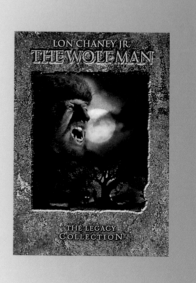

LON CHANEY JR.
THE WOLF MAN

THE LEGACY COLLECTION

p.45
p.195
p.14
p.378

Library Association selected *The Silver Kiss* as one of its hundred **Best of the Best Books** in 1994. *Alien Secrets* was a *Booklist* **Best Book** and a *School Library Journal* **Best Book** in 1993. *Blood and Chocolate* won those same honors in 1997.

Annette Curtis Klause's books are sometimes controversial. Even after it won the 2000 **Young Adult Book Award** from the **South Carolina Association of School Librarians**, *Blood and Chocolate* was removed from the middle school libraries of Greenville because of protests from a few teachers and parents.

– Faith Hickman Brynie

South Carolina Association of School Librarians

The state association of school librarians in South Carolina sponsors an annual book award program. Teachers, students, media specialists, parents, administrators, public librarians, and college and university representatives agree to serve a three-year term on the selection committee. During the year they read 100 to 150 books and discuss and evaluate them with the other committee members. The result is a list of nominees for the best book in three categories: for children, juniors, and young adults. From the lists, one book is selected as Book Award in each category.

E. L. Konigsburg

Born: February 10, 1930; New York, New York

www.eduplace.com/kids/hmr/mtai/konigsburg.html

E. L. Konigsburg's novels range from the amusing *From the Mixed-Up Files of Mrs. Basil E. Frankweiler*, to the wrenching *Silent to the Bone*. In all her books, however, readers can rely upon her for sharp characterizations, strong insights, and a keen sympathy for young people. Konigsburg never sugar-coats anything. For example, *The View from Saturday* suggests what many readers probably suspect—that young trouble-makers often become old trouble-makers, while wise young souls grow into their wisdom. Endings therefore often depend upon beginnings.

Born Elaine Lobel in New York City, Konigsburg was raised in small Pennsylvania towns. A talented artist, voracious reader, and excellent student, she graduated at the top of her high school class. As the first person in her family to attend college, she lacked the kind of family support and guidance that many young people today take for granted. To pay for her schooling, she planned to work full time and attend college in alternate years. Fortunately, upon enrolling at Carnegie Mellon University, she met an English professor who heard her plan and helped her obtain academic **scholarships**. p.380 In this way, Konigsburg was able to remain at the university, pursuing her studies in chemistry.

After graduating with honors, she married David Konigsburg, the brother of a former employer, and began graduate work in chemistry. When she and her husband moved to Jacksonville, Florida, she

TITLES

From the Mixed-Up Files of Mrs. Basil E. Frankweiler, 1967

The View from Saturday, 1996

Silent to the Bone, 2000

The Outcasts of 19 Schuyler Place, 2004

Scholarships

Scholarships provide financial assistance to students attending school or college. A scholarship may be given because of need or because of achievement. Interested students must apply for a scholarship. The application is then evaluated by a committee and the most deserving applicants are selected to receive assistance. For many poor students, scholarships are the only way to pay for a higher education. For those who excel in academics or sports, it is a way to be rewarded for their hard work and skill.

became a chemistry teacher at a private all-girl's school. The experience gave her important insights into the lives of young people who, despite their money and privilege, were as uncertain about their lives as she had been. She soon left teaching to rear a family. One day, while her family was on a picnic, her children complained so much about the heat, ants, and hardness of the ground, she thought that should her children ever run away from home, they would need to find some place really elegant and comfortable, such as the Metropolitan Museum of Art, in which to live. These thoughts led to her first novel. p.381

From the Mixed-Up Files of Mrs. Basil E. Frankweiler tells the stories of two suburban children who do precisely what Konigsburg imagined. Claudia Kincaid, tired of her boring life as the older sister of three brothers, decides to teach her parents a lesson in "Claudia appreciation." Taking along her least objectionable brother—both for his company and for his savings, she runs off. While hiding in the Metropolitan Museum of Art, she and her brother discover a mystery about the origins of a statue. Claudia guesses that solving the mystery of who created the sculpture will help her discover who *she* is. Her quest leads her to Mrs. Basil E. Frankweiler, the narrator of the story.

Konigsburg's later novels, *The View from Saturday* and *Silent to the Bone*, also deal with discovering who one is, once one has stripped away the clutter of past achievements, mistakes, and difficulties. Both novels have earned critical praise and devoted readers.

p.102 E. L. Konigsburg's books have received many honors, including **Newbery Medals** for both *From the Mixed-Up Files of Mrs. Basil E. Frankweiler* and *The View from Saturday*.

– Angela M. Salas

Metropolitan Museum of Art

The Met, as it is commonly called, is one of the world's great art museums. It is located in New York City. Founded in 1870, the museum was moved from its original location to Central Park in 1880. The museum faces Fifth Avenue, and its current entrance was built in 1926. Additions to the original building now completely surround it. Its collection now contains more than two million pieces of art from the ancient world to modern times. The museum's collections continue to grow through purchases and through donations by art collectors.

Dean Ray Koontz

Born: July 9, 1945; Everett, Pennsylvania

deankoontz.com

Dean R. Koontz has published more than eighty novels and sold more than 200 million copies of his books. His work has been translated into thirty-eight languages. Not only is he prolific, he is one of the most versatile writers of our time and has written in almost every imaginable genre. Throughout all his fiction, however, love, friendship, and a commitment to freedom enable characters to defeat their enemies and control their destinies.

Dean Koontz grew up in a small, rural town in Pennsylvania. His father, an alcoholic given to violent outbursts, provided little security, going through forty-four jobs in thirty-four years. Koontz's mother tried to shield her son from his father's rage, but the boy's best refuge was in books, movies, and storytelling. When he was only eight years old, he taped his stories together and sold them as books for a nickel each. At the age of twelve, he won a nationwide newspaper contest for an essay on the theme of "What Being an American Means to Me."

p.10

While attending Pennsylvania's Shippensburg State College, Koontz won the *Atlantic Monthly* competition for a short story and began selling his fiction. After graduating in 1966, he married Gerda Ann Cerra and worked as a teacher-counselor in the Appalachian Poverty Program. Disillusioned with government inefficiency after only a year, he shifted to teaching high school English, while continuing to write and publish science-fiction novels. A year and a half later, he began writing full time. In only four years, he was earning enough from

p.383

his writing to allow Gerda to quit her job.

Koontz began experimenting with a variety of genres in 1971, using for each a different writing style and pseudonym. He wrote crime-suspense novels as Deanna Dwyer, thrillers as Brian Coffey, adventure stories as John Hill, and other genres under other pen names. In 1976 he began writing cross-genre novels that combined suspense, romance, humor, magic, and the supernatural. In *Watchers*, a botched experiment in a government lab produces two mutants. One of them, a cross between an ape and a dog, becomes a killer; the other, an intelligent golden retriever named Einstein, becomes a spy. In *Lightning* a woman is protected by a stranger throughout her life before learning that he is a time-traveler pursued by killers from his past.

In 1966 Koontz won the *Atlantic Monthly* **Creative Writing Award** for his short story "Kittens," and in 1971, *Beastchild* was nominated for a **Hugo Award**. Eight of his novels have risen to number one on the *New York Times* hardcover **best-seller list**, and eleven of his books in paperback have reached the number one position. *Watchers* was selected as

Atlantic Monthly

Previously known as *The Atlantic*, this American monthly magazine publishes articles on social and cultural issues. The articles are written by writers who are known for the quality of their writing and their intelligence. The magazine covers recent history, humor, fiction, poetry, the arts, and book reviews. It was founded in 1857 and continues to be a thought-provoking publication.

Best-seller Lists

Best-seller lists are published by many newspapers and magazines. They list current books in order of the number of books sold. They are very important to publishers because a book's appearance on a best-seller list will encourage more readers to buy the book. *The New York Times* publishes one of the most respected best-seller lists. The list ranks books based on a poll of some 4,000 bookstores and major wholesellers who provide books to some 60,000 other outlets. *Publishers Weekly* magazine also publishes an influential best-seller list compiled from data received from independent and chain bookstores.

PUBLISHERS WEEKLY

Available online the Friday before issue date at: www.publishersweekly.com

October 18, 2004

Hardcover Bestsellers

Fiction

		LAST WEEK	WEEKS ON LIST
1	**The Dark Tower VII: The Dark Tower.** *Stephen King.* Scribner/Grant, $35 ISBN 1-880418-62-2	1	3
2	**The Plot Against America.** *Philip Roth.* Houghton Mifflin, $26 ISBN 0-618-50928-3	8	3
3	**The Da Vinci Code.** *Dan Brown.* Doubleday, $24.95 ISBN 0-385-50420-9	3	81
4	**Incubus Dreams.** *Laurell K. Hamilton.* Berkley, $23.95 ISBN 0-425-19824-3	2	2
5	**Trace.** *Patricia Cornwell.* Putnam, $26.95 ISBN 0-399-15219-9	4	5
6	**Shopaholic & Sister.** *Sophie Kinsella.* Dial, $23 ISBN 0-385-33809-0	6	2
7	**The Five People You Meet in Heaven.** *Mitch Albom.* Hyperion, $19.95 ISBN 0-7868-6871-6	5	54
8	**Jonathan Strange & Mr. Norrell.** *Susanna Clarke.* Bloomsbury, $27.95 ISBN 1-58234-416-7	7	6
9	**Nights of Rain and Stars.** *Maeve Binchy.* Dutton, $25.95 ISBN 0-525-94754-X	9	3
10	**Are You Afraid of the Dark?** *Sidney Sheldon.* Morrow, $25 ISBN 0-06-059934-9	10	4
11	**The Sunday Philosophy Club.** *Alexander McCall Smith.* Pantheon, $19.95 ISBN 0-375-42298-6	11	2
12	**The Rule of Four.** *Ian Caldwell and Dustin Thomason.* Dial, $24 ISBN 0-385-33711-6	12	22
13	**Little Earthquakes.** *Jennifer Weiner.* Atria, $26 ISBN 0-7434-7009-5	13	4
14	**Double Homicide: Santa Fe.** *Jonathan and Faye Kellerman.* Warner, $23.95 ISBN 0-446-53296-7	–	1
15	**Melancholy Baby.** *Robert B. Parker.* Putnam, $24.95 ISBN 0-399-15218-0	14	2

Nonfiction

		LAST WEEK	WEEKS ON LIST
1	**America (The Book).** *Jon Stewart, Ben Karlin and David Javerbaum.* Warner, $24.95 ISBN 0-446-53268-1	1	3
2	**He's Just Not That Into You.** *Greg Behrendt and Liz Tuccillo.* Simon Spotlight Entertainment, $19.95 ISBN 0-689-87474-X	2	3
3	**How to Talk to a Liberal (If You Must):The World According to Ann Coulter.** *Ann Coulter.* Crown Forum, $26.95 ISBN 1-4000-5418-4	–	1
4	**Chronicles: Volume One.** *Bob Dylan.* Simon & Schuster, $24 ISBN 0-7432-2815-4	–	1
5	**The South Beach Diet.** *Arthur Agatston, M.D.* Rodale, $24.95 ISBN 1-57954-646-3	4	78
6	**The Purpose-Driven Life.** *Rick Warren.* Zondervan, $19.99 ISBN 0-310-20571-9	7	88
7	**Family First: Your Step-by-Step Plan for Creating a Phenomenal Family.** *Dr. Phil McGraw.* Free Press, $26 ISBN 0-7432-6493-2	3	4
8	**Unfit for Command: Swift Boat Veterans Speak Out Against John Kerry.** *John E. O'Neill & Jerome R. Corsi.* Regnery, $27.95 ISBN 0-89526-017-4	5	9
9	**Will They Ever Trust Us Again?: Letters from the War Zone.** *Michael Moore.* Simon & Schuster, $22 ISBN 0-7432-7152-1	–	1
10	**The Family: The Real Story of the Bush Dynasty.** *Kitty Kelley.* Doubleday, $29.95 ISBN 0-385-50324-5	6	4
11	**The Gourmet Cookbook.** Edited by *Ruth Reichl.* Houghton Mifflin, $40 ISBN 0-618-37408-6	8	2
12	**Eats, Shoots & Leaves.** *Lynne Truss.* Gotham, $17.50 ISBN 1-592-40087-6	9	26
13	**Shadow War: The Untold Story of How Bush Is Winning the War on Terror.** *Richard Miniter.* Regnery, $27.95 ISBN 0-89526-052-2	–	1
14	**Between a Rock and a Hard Place.** *Aron Ralston.* Atria, $26 ISBN 0-7434-9281-1	11	5
15	**Chain of Command: The Road from 9/11 to Abu Ghraib.** *Seymour M. Hersh.* HarperCollins, $25.95 ISBN 0-06-019591-6	10	4

Compiled from data received from independent and chain bookstores. Copyright ©2004 by Publishers Weekly. The lists may not be reproduced without permission from the publisher.

p.480
p.4[

a **Best Book for Young Adults** by the **American Library Association** in 1987, and *Twilight Eyes* won a **Daedalus Award** in 1988. *Lightning* and *Oddkins* were placed on the Youth-to-Youth reading list by the Young Adult Advisory Board of the Enoch Pratt Free Library.

Koontz wrote and produced *The Face of Fear* for television and a screenplay of *Cold Fire*, *Midnight*, and *Phantoms*. Several of his novels have been made into movies, including *Demon Seed*, *Shattered*, *The Funhouse*, *Watchers*, and *Hideaway*, and *Intensity*, *Sole Survivor*, and *Mr. Murder* have all become television miniseries. In 1989 he received an **honorary doctorate** from Shippensburg State College.

p.204

– Bernard E. Morris

Kathryn Lasky

Born: June 24, 1944; Indianapolis, Indiana

www.kathrynlasky.com/newfilm/homelsk.htm

Kathryn Lasky is best known for the variety of her publications, which include nonfiction picture books, biographies, novels for young adults, and **historical novels**. She has also written photographic essays in collaboration with her husband, photographer Christopher Knight. Her chief interest as writer lies in her ability to tell a good story, even in her works of nonfiction. As a child she found nonfiction books to be boring and dry, so as a writer she has tried to make her own nonfiction books as readable as her fiction.

p.117

Born in Indianapolis, Indiana, Lasky graduated from the University of Michigan in 1966 with a degree in English. She earned a master's degree from Wheelock College in Massachusetts in 1977. After graduating from Michigan, she wrote for magazines and worked as a teacher. She married Christopher Knight in 1971 and published her first book in 1975. Her wide-ranging interests have taken her throughout the world to sheep-shearing farms, **archaeological digs**, and a sailboat crossing the Atlantic.

p.83

Lasky's own real-life experiences and those of her family inspire much of her work. For example, *Marven of the Great North Woods* is based on her father's childhood experiences, and *The Night Journey* is based on her grandmother's family experiences. *The Night Journey* tells the story of Nana Sashie, as she relates it to her thirteen-year-old

TITLES

The Night Journey, 1981

Beyond the Divide, 1983

The Bone Wars, 1988

Beyond the Burning Time, 1994

Memoirs of a Bookbat, 1994

Marven of the Great North Woods, 1997

Blood Secret, 2004

Czarist Russia

The coronation of Ivan IV, also called Ivan the Terrible, as czar or emperor of Russia on January 16, 1547, was a major change in rulership in Russia. Until then the rulers of Russia had been called princes, a designation that defined authority over a particular principality. However, when Ivan IV

stepped in as czar, he conquered the remaining independent principalities, thus becoming ruler of the entire country. The last czar to rule Russia was Nicholas II, who abdicated the crown in 1917, so ending Czarist Russia and ushering in Communist Russia.

great-granddaughter, Rachel. Rachel learns the exciting story of how Sashie's family escaped from **czarist Russia** with the help of a plan devised by Sashie, who was a child at the time.

p.38

Beyond the Divide is set in America in 1849. In that story, a fourteen-year-old Amish girl leaves her home in Pennsylvania to travel across the continent by wagon train with her father, who has been shunned by the Amish community. They gain some measure of acceptance within the wagon train community, but when the girl's father is injured, both of them are left behind to fend for themselves. Another historical novel, *Beyond the Burning Time* deals with accusations of **witchcraft** in 1691 **New England** as a twelve-year-old girl fights to save her mother from execution.

p.320

p.63

In *Marven of the Great North Woods* ten-year-old Marven must leave home when the **1919 influenza epidemic** strikes Duluth, Minnesota. To escape the epidemic, his parents send him to a logging camp in the great north woods. Alone in a foreign environment, not knowing if he will ever see his parents again, Marven befriends a physically intimidating, yet kind, lumberjack and begins to adjust to his new environment.

p.38

Lasky treats the subject of censorship in *Memoirs of a Bookbat*. This is the story of a fourteen-year-old fantasy-fiction fan who is forced to hide her books from her fundamentalist parents. The girl must question her parents' religious views on censorship when her own freedom is threatened.

p.87

Kathryn Lasky's writing honors include the **National Jewish Book Award** for children for *Night Journey*, the American Library Association **Best Books for Young Adults** for *Beyond the Burning*, and the Boston Globe-Horn Book Award for nonfiction for *The Weaver's Gift* (1981). She also received the **Washington Post-Children's Book Guild Award** for her contributions to children's nonfiction.

p.45
480
p.747

– Mary Virginia Davis

Influenza Epidemic of 1919

Influenza, or "flu," is an illness caused by a virus. Many people become ill each year with influenza because the virus mutates, or changes, from year to year. In general, only the very young and the very old are at risk for serious complications; today, vaccinations exist that offer protection against

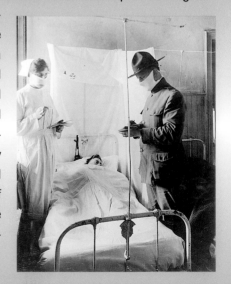

flu viruses. However, back in 1918, a deadly strain of influenza surfaced, quickly spreading throughout the world. Although symptoms associated with influenza are usually not worse than those associated with a bad cold, the 1918 virus caused bleeding from the nose and the lungs. People exposed to the disease were dead within three days. The worldwide influenza epidemic finally ended in the spring of 1919, leaving at least thirty million people dead. World longevity statistics dipped sharply for the year. Birthrates plummeted because of the large numbers of young women who had died. The influenza was all the more catastrophic because it followed hard on the devastation wrought by World War I.

Iain Lawrence

Born: February 25, 1955; Sault Ste. Marie, Ontario, Canada

www.randomhouse.com/features/iainlawrence

Sailing and the sea form the backdrop for most of **Iain Lawrence**'s adventure stories. Many of his characters are young boys who find adventure and danger and must outwit nature and enemies in battles between good and evil.

Lawrence was born in northern Ontario, Canada, and his family moved eleven times before he left high school. He acquired a love of reading from listening to bedtime stories read by his father, and the first books he wrote as a youngster were storybooks for his younger brother. Early in his writing career, he had to support himself with many different odd jobs because no one would buy his short stories. Finally he decided to study journalism and he spent ten years writing for newspapers in northern British Columbia. Lawrence eventually quit his job to try creative writing again, supporting himself by working on a fish farm. His first novel was about

a shipwrecked boy who was captured by wreckers, but again, he could not find anyone to publish it. Finally Lawrence's agent suggested that he rewrite *The Wreckers* as a novel for younger readers, and the novel sold within a month.

The Wreckers became the first book in Lawrence's High Seas trilogy,

Albino

Albinism is a rare genetic condition characterized by a lack of skin pigmentation, pale hair, and eyes with a pink or blue iris and red pupil. Whites affected with albinism have extremely pale skin and white or yellow hair, and blacks with the defect have very light brown skin and hair that is white, slightly yellow, or yellowish brown. Albinos with a less severe form of the disorder may experience some darkening of the skin and hair with age. Albinism causes such eye problems as myopia (nearsightedness), squinting, and photophobia (dislike of bright light), but its main danger is to the skin: Albinos have no melanin, a brown skin pigment, to protect them from the sun's harmful radiation, and often develop skin cancers.

a series that centers on the adventures of young John Spencer. The "Wreckers" of its title are people in a village on the coast of Cornwall, England, who live off the wreckage of ships that crash on their rocky shore. Fourteen-year-old John Spencer is the only survivor of the wreck of the ship *The Isle of Skye*; now he must survive the murderous wreckers. The second book, *The Smugglers*, finds John sailing the seas in his own schooner *The Dragon*, facing the unknown in a boat that may be cursed. In the final book of the series, *The Buccaneers*, seventeen-year-old John is again sailing *The Dragon*. He finds adventure and danger on his first voyage to foreign lands.

A fourteen-year-old albino boy named Harold Kline is the main character in *Ghost Boy*. He finds his adventure on solid ground. Tired of being taunted and stared at because he is an albino, he runs off to join the circus. Ten-year-old Johnny, the *Lord of the Nutcracker Men*, enjoys playing war games with the nutcracker soldiers made for him by his father in this historical novel set during World War I. When his father enlists to fight in France,

Geoffrey Bilson Historical Fiction Award

In 1988, the Geoffrey Bilson Historical Fiction Award was established in memory of Geoffrey Bilson, a respected historian and children's author. The award includes an annual prize of $1,000 that is awarded to a Canadian author who has demonstrated outstanding work in historical fiction for young people. The award is given based on the decision of the jury selected by the Canadian Children's Book Centre.

however, Johnny learns that war is not a game. In *The Lightkeeper's Daughter*, seventeen-year-old Squid McCrae returns to Lizzie Island to confront her parents and painful memories of the past.

Iain Lawrence's novels have won many awards, including four American Library Association Best Books for Young Adults awards and the Geoffrey Bilson Historical Fiction Award for *The Wreckers*.

p.480

p.4

p.39

– Deborah DePiero

Harper Lee

Born: April 28, 1926; Monroeville, Alabama

mockingbird.chebucto.org

Harper Lee's only novel, *To Kill a Mockingbird*, is written from the vantage point of an adult, vividly recalling her childhood in a small southern town. After their mother's death, the **protagonist** and her older brother are reared by their father, Atticus Finch, a respected attorney and a role model for his children.

Born Nelle Harper Lee, the author grew up in Monroeville, Alabama. Her father, Amasa Coleman Lee, was a prominent lawyer, legislator, and newspaperman. Her mother, Frances Finch Lee, was a member of an old southern family. Harper had two sisters and a brother. One of their playmates was Truman Streckfus Persons, who would later become famous as author **Truman Capote**. Harper was an imaginative child; she read widely and by the time she was seven was beginning to write.

Lee attended public schools in Monroeville then spent a year at Huntington College in Montgomery, Alabama, before transferring in 1945 to the University of Alabama. There she spent four years, including one as an exchange student at **Oxford University** in England. During her college years, Lee often contributed to campus publications. Six months before she was to obtain her law degree,

p.233

392

p.173

TITLE

To Kill a Mockingbird, 1960

as her father had expected, she left the university and moved to New York. There she supported herself by working as an airline-reservations clerk until a literary agent urged her to expand one of her short stories into a novel. Lee promptly quit her job and spent all her time writing what became *To Kill a Mockingbird*.

The novel is based on places and people Lee knew well. Not only does the fictional town of Maycomb, Alabama, closely resemble Monroeville, but Lee has also pointed out that her town's school playground, the old, "haunted" house, and the courtroom all appear in her novel. The young boy called Charles Baker Harris, or "Dill," was modeled on their friend, the future Truman Capote, and Harper Lee's father was the inspiration for the similarly courageous lawyer Atticus Finch.

To Kill a Mockingbird is best known as the story of a white lawyer who defends an African American man falsely accused of assaulting a young white girl in a community that will not even consider the possibility of a black man's innocence. However, there are several other incidents in the novel, unrelated to race, that demonstrate how wrong it is to make judgments about people based on external appearances. The novel also questions society's imposition

Truman Capote

Truman Streckfus Persons was born in New Orleans, September 30, 1924, to Lillie Mae Faulk (later changed to Nina) and Arch Persons. After his parents' divorce and his mother's remarriage, Truman took the surname of his adoptive stepfather and became known only as Truman Capote. He was a childhood friend of Harper Lee; the character Dill in *To Kill a Mockingbird* was based on him. However, despite the lighthearted and happy nature of Dill, Truman had an unhappy and lonely childhood, which became the subject of much of his work. His sense of abandonment and betrayal remained with him throughout his life.

To Kill a Mockingbird, the Movie

its

Released in 1962, *To Kill a Mockingbird* quickly won over audiences for it's accurate portrayal of racial injustice in the American South, it's faithfulness to the best-selling novel by Harper Lee, and its award-winning performances. In light of the Civil Rights movement in America, *To Kill a Mockingbird* worked to portray the indecency of the plight of African Americans and the problem of injustice as a part of life. However, the movie's greatest asset was its portrayal of the injustice through the eyes of a child. The innocence of the young characters evoked emotion in the audience. This, in combination with the strong acting performances, provided the strength behind the movie's success.

of gender roles, as the tomboy narrator, Jean Louise ("Scout") Finch, resists her aunt's attempts to transform her into a southern lady.

Harper Lee's first novel was a **best-seller** and a critical success; in 1961, it won the **Pulitzer Prize**. The **film** *To Kill a Mockingbird* (1962) is now itself considered a classic. Because of its artistry and its p.393 timeless theme, the book has remained popular with readers of all ages. It is frequently assigned in high school and college classes.

Although Harper Lee spoke of writing another novel, one has not appeared. She lives a quiet life in New York and Monroeville, seldom granting interviews or making public appearances.

— Rosemary M. Canfield Reisman

Ursula K. Le Guin

Born: October 21, 1929; Berkeley, California

www.ursulakleguin.com

Ursula K. Le Guin's writing is strongly influenced by her family's academic background. She is the daughter of the famous anthropologist Alfred Kroeber and writer and psychologist Theodora Kroeber. She herself studied Renaissance history and married a history professor. Her father had been a student of Franz Boas, the founder of the school of cultural relativism in anthropology. The open-minded attitude to other cultures that Le Guin grew up with imbues her fictional depictions of alternate worlds and realities. Le Guin's work has been criticized by some fundamentalist Christians as advocating "foreign religions," and she describes herself as a Taoist. However, the religions in her p.39 fiction appear as natural aspects of alien cultures; she does not push a religious agenda but a philosophical one.

Le Guin started reading science fiction at an early age, and her first novels were in that genre, set in the far-distant future of a place recognizably related to the present-day Earth. Le Guin initially wrote in the space-opera genre, but even then her characters' heroics were tempered with deeper concerns of the importance of communication and a critique of authoritarianism. Her later science fiction, such as *The Lathe of Heaven*, delves into exploration of gender roles and **androgyny** as well. The stories p.55 taking place in her science-fiction universe are known as the Hainish cycle, including *Rocannon's World*, *Planet of Exile*, *City of Illusions*, *The Dispossessed*, *The Lathe of Heaven*, and *The Telling*. (Hain is the planet that was the source of human life on Earth, as well as on other planets.)

Le Guin's best-known works are the Earthsea cycle: *A Wizard of Earthsea*, *The Tombs of Atuan*, *The Farthest Shore*, *Tehanu*, *Tales from Earthsea* and *The Other Wind*. Her creation of the world of Earthsea has been compared to J. R. R. Tolkien's Middle-earth. Interestingly, both Le Guin and **Tolkien** were steeped not only in mythology as narrative, but also in the academic study of mythology. Le Guin's Earthsea books recount the life of Ged, a member of the all-male order of wizards that maintains the rule of Earthsea through magic. One of the significant ways in which Le Guin departs from many of the conventions of **fantasy** writing is in her unabashed feminism; Ged, for instance, breaks **patriarchy's** hold on the governance of the world and on the understanding of magic. While *Tehanu* questions Le Guin's initial assumptions about the relationship between gender and magic, *The Other Wind* questions assumptions about the relationship between magic and life and death.

One of the strengths of Le Guin's long writing career is that her ideas about society, culture, and

104
.87
96

Taoism

Taoism, also known as Daoism, is a philosophy that involves ethics, metaphysics, and political philosophy. A vague notion of the *dao* existed in ancient China long before any Taoists or Mohists or Confucians expounded their respective views on this concept. It stemmed, apparently, from an early effort of the Chinese mind to search into the mystery of the universe and to discover the rationale, if any, behind things. To name the unnamable, the Chinese borrowed this term, *dao*, or the Way. The ambiguous nature of this term allows it to serve several doctrines. Hence, to Confucious, *dao* means the Sage Kings way to social harmony; to Mozi, *dao* means the way to an ample supply of staple foods and a populous state; and to Mencius, *dao* means the way to moral (and spiritual) perfection. However, to a Taoist, *dao* could mean all these and more.

especially gender have changed over time. This evolution is evident in her writing. Unlike other "genre" novelists who essentially write the same story over and over because their fans take comfort in it, Le Guin challenges her readers by revealing new perspectives that may undercut the assumptions on which her previous novels were based—much as, in the field of anthropology, new perspectives may make older ethnographies of a culture appear dated or outright wrong.

In addition to awards within the field of science fiction that Le Guin has received, she has received a number of awards within the field of young adult literature. *A Wizard of Earthsea* won a **Boston Globe-Horn Book** p.74 **Award**, *The Farthest Shore* won a **National Book** p.122 **Award**, and *The Tombs of Atuan* received both a **Newberry Honor Book** and a **Phoenix Honor** p. **Award**.

— Leslie Ellen Jones

Patriarchy

Patriarchy is a family organization consistent with the cultural traditions of pastoral peoples. Men have absolute and final authority in their households. Women are married into their husbands' families, and children inherit their fathers' names. Traditionally, patriarchal societies preferred male children, because they were more useful than females for hard, pastoral work and warfare. Women's primary role was to be men's helpmates. Patriarchy has come to dominate Western attitudes toward sexuality and the family. Women in patriarchal cultures are considered men's property. Because of the chattel status of women in such cultures, men and women who have violated the same taboo may be guilty of different crimes. According to ancient Jewish law, for example, men who committed adultery were guilty of stealing others men's property, which was not a capital offense. Women accused of committing adultery, however, could be punished by death.

Madeleine L'Engle

Born: November 29, 1918; New York, New York

www.madeleinelengle.com

p.87

p.102

Madeleine L'Engle is a prolific writer in many genres but is best known for her fifteen science-fiction and fantasy novels for young adults. She has won numerous awards, including a Newbery Medal for *A Wrinkle in Time*, while *A Ring of Endless Light* was a **Newbery Honor Book**. Her individual books started out as members of separate series, but over the years her characters have jumped from one series to another so often that it is better to think of her novels as all taking place in a single fictional universe, even though the novels about the Austin family tend to be more concerned with the real world and the novels about the Murry and O'Keefe family contain more traveling through time and space.

L'Engle was born in New York City, the only child of Charles Wadsworth Camp, a writer who was a veteran of World War I, and Madeleine Barnett Camp, a pianist. Her father had suffered lung damage in the war that caused ongoing health problems. As a result, L'Engle spent much of her childhood either alone—creating for herself a vivid fantasy life—and at p.168 **boarding school** while her parents went to Switzerland for her father's health. Her father died while she was still at school. She at-

TITLES

Meet the Austins, 1960

A Wrinkle in Time, 1962

The Moon by Night, 1963

The Twenty-four Days Before Christmas: An Austin Family Story, 1964

The Arm of the Starfish, 1965

The Young Unicorns, 1968

A Wind in the Door, 1973

Dragons in the Waters, 1976

A Swiftly Tilting Planet, 1978

A Ring of Endless Light, 1980

The Anti-Muffins, 1981

A House Like a Lotus, 1984

Many Waters, 1986

An Acceptable Time, 1989

A Full House: An Austin Family Christmas, 1999

Smith College

As the nation's largest liberal arts college for women, Smith College offers a variety of academic, cultural, and social advantages. Founded in 1871, Smith College began as the dream of one woman who wanted to provide a quality education for women that would be equal to that offered for men. After inheriting a large fortune at the age of 65, Sophia Smith made the decision to invest her money in an institution rooted in tradition that would help to further the role and influence of women in society. Although Smith College has changed over time, it has remained constant in fulfilling the dream of Sophia Smith by offering exceptional resources and facilities, a dedicated faculty and staff, and an outstanding international curriculum. Located in Northhampton, Massachusetts, Smith College remains a symbol of the accomplishments of women in society.

p.398 tended **Smith College** and there became involved in theater. For several years after graduation, she worked in theater, serving as assistant stage manager of a production of Anton Chekov's play *The Cherry Orchard* (1904) and in the process met and married actor Hugh Franklin. They spent a few years running a country store in rural Connecticut as they started their family, then returned to New York City. Franklin eventually landed a long-running role on the soap opera *All My Children*. He died in 1986.

It was difficult for L'Engle to get her early novels published. Twenty-six different publishers rejected *A Wrinkle in Time* before it was accepted by **Farrar, Straus and Giroux**. The problem was that her work did not fit clearly in either the kind of clas-

p.399

sic hard science fiction set on spaceships and other planets or in classic fantasy set in alternate realities that relies on magic rather than science.

The families at the center of Madeleine L'Engle's novels are scientists, but usually biologists rather than physicists or engineers. Although science propels her plots, her stories are concerned with **ethical** and spiritual questions that go far beyond the social responsibility to use science wisely. Characters may have to deal with threats from a malign disembodied brain or with **homosexual** advances from a formerly trusted friend. L'Engle is a **Christian** and her values strongly color her work without becoming dogmatic or preachy.

 p.10

p.57

p.410

— Leslie Ellen Jones

Farrar, Straus and Giroux

As part of a growing publishing industry, Farrar, Straus and Giroux stands apart for its renowned list of literary fiction, nonfiction, poetry, and children's books. Founded in 1946 by Roger M. Straus, the company has been home to a variety of award-winning authors including T.S. Eliot, Joseph Brodsky, William Golding, Pablo Neruda, and Derek Walcott. Farrar, Straus and Giroux also publishes the North Point Press, Hill and Wang, and Faber and Faber imprints and distributes Aperture, Graywolf Press, and Enchanted Lion Press books. Located in New York, Farrar, Straus and Giroux continues to be an important influence in the publishing world.

 FARRAR, STRAUS AND GIROUX

Julius Lester

Born: January 27, 1939; St. Louis, Missouri

www.childrenslit.com/f_lester.html

Julius Lester has reworked and updated several traditional folktales, including Little Black Sambo and the Uncle Remus stories to make them more acceptable to modern readers. However, he is not afraid to tackle controversial, complex subject matter and challenge perceptions about race. He has taken on topics as lighthearted as the alliterative fables in *Ackamarackus* (2001) for young readers as well as the provocative and thought-provoking themes found in *When Dad Killed Mom* for young adults. Whatever his audience or subject matter, his work is always vital, vibrant and challenging.

The son of a Methodist minister, Lester grew up wanting to be a musician in the seg-regated South of the 1940's and 1950's. After graduating from Fisk University with a degree in English, he became active in the Civil Rights movement. He also pursued a career in music, writing songs, recording two albums, and coauthoring a book with folksinger Pete Seeger. He produced and hosted a radio program in New York City for eight years and hosted a live television show. During that period he also published many books for adults. On the advice of his publisher, he began writing children's literature, publishing his first children's book, *To Be a Slave*, in 1969. He joined the faculty of the University of Massachusetts at Amherst in 1971.

In *Sam and the Tigers*, Lester re-imagines Helen Bannerman's *Little Black Sambo*, re-

p.40

p.66

p.40

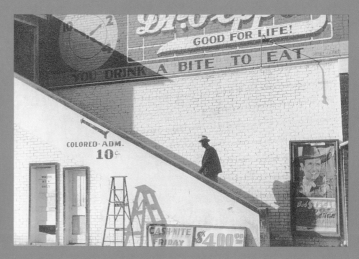

Segregation

Segregation of minorities in the United States was a negative social and economic practice that kept the country from achieving "liberty, freedom, and equality," promises upon which the nation was founded. American segregation was born in the colonial era, when most blacks were slaves. This resulted in free blacks also being segregated in housing and social life based on custom and folkways. After the Civil War, states passed laws making segregation legal. In *Plessy v. Ferguson*, the Supreme Court ruled that segregation was legal as long as "separate but equal" facilities were available for minorities. In 1954 the Supreme Court declared segregated public education illegal. Ten years later the passage of the Civil Rights Act of of 1964 brought a legal end to segregation.

placing the now racially charged name Sambo with Sam, and in fact creating a land, Sam-sam-samara, in which all of the characters are called Sam. Lester's Sam is sassy, street-wise and hip, giving an old story a refreshing new life. Lester also tackles the Uncle Remus tales, which he retells in five volumes, *The Tales of Uncle Remus* (1987), *More Tales of Uncle Remus* (1988), *Further Tales of Uncle Remus* (1990), *The Last Tales of Uncle Remus* (1994), and *Uncle Remus*. Again, he breathes new life into these old African American folktales and makes them acceptable to a contemporary audience.

In a more serious vein, Lester reworks William Shakespeare's play *Othello* (1604), removing race as an issue by making the characters of Desdemona and Iago black. He also transforms the biblical story of Moses in *Pharaoh's Daughter*, bringing new life to an ancient story by telling it from the point of view of a teenage Moses. *When Dad Killed Mom* is a contemporary story about two children whose mother is

Pete Seeger

Pete Seeger was born May 3, 1919, into a very musical family; his father Charles, was a musicologist and a professor at the University of California at Berkeley, and his mother was a pianist. From an early age he loved to sing, and later he learned to play the banjo. In 1941, he met Lee Hays, and together they founded the Almanac Singers. When Pete was drafted in 1942, the Almanac Singers disbanded. After he was discharged from the army in 1949, he founded a new group, the Weavers. After the breakup of the Weavers, he traveled around the country appearing at high schools and small auditoriums. He was known mainly for his political views which often caused widespread controversy. He became deeply involved in the civil rights protests of the 1960's and even appeared in Birmingham, Alabama in 1963 when civil rights leader Martin Luther King, Jr., was in prison. Seeger was the one to bring the song "We Shall Overcome" to the attention of civil rights groups, and he sang the song, adding verses, all through this difficult period.

murdered by their father. The point of view alternates between Jeremy and his older, eighth-grade sister Jenna. Written for older children and teenagers, this powerful story explores the children's complicated feelings and their struggle to make sense of their chaotic lives.

Julius Lester has received numerous honors in his career, including the **Newbery Honor Book** award for *To Be a Slave* and two American Library Association **Best Books for Young Adults** awards. He has also received many honors for his teaching work, including the Massachusetts State Professor of the Year.

– Mary Virginia Davis

p.1
p.4
p.48

Gail Carson Levine

Born: September 17, 1947; New York, New York

www.harperchildrens.com/hch/author/author/levine

Although **Gail Carson Levine**'s novels are published and marketed as children's books, many of them contain strong teenage characters who appeal to audiences of all ages, including young adults who still enjoy fairy tales. The wide-ranging appeal of her books has been recognized by the American Library Association, which has honored Levine with awards in both its Best Books for Young Adults and its **Notable Books for Younger Readers** categories.

With a father who owned a commercial art studio and a mother who wrote plays for her students to perform, Levine was raised in a creative family. Her first ambition was to be a painter like her older sister, who became an art professor. After earning her bachelor's degree at the City College of New York in 1969, Levine worked for twenty-seven years in the field of social welfare as an employment interviewer and administrator. Along the way she continued practicing and learning about art. She also took a class in writing and illustrating children's books. It was only then that she discovered how much she preferred writing to painting.

For an assignment in another class, Levine started writing *Ella Enchanted*, a feisty Cinderella story that she finished on the train while commuting to and from her job. However, it would be nine years before her first book would be published—a wait with a fairy-tale reward at the end, as *Ella En-*

p.45

480

p.404

TITLES

Ella Enchanted, 1997

Dave at Night, 1999

The Wish, 2000

The Two Princesses of Bamarre, 2001

chanted was named a **Newbery Honor Book** after it was published. It went on to win other awards, including readers-choice awards in several states. This adaptation of Cinderella has a unique twist: Ella is not a goody-goody character by choice. When she was born, a foolish fairy bestowed upon her a gift of obedience that requires her to obey all commands. The plot creatively builds on the traditional threads and maintains suspense until its happy ending.

After her success with *Ella Enchanted*, Levine soon went on to publish The Princess Tales, a popular series of fairy-tale adaptations for children. Another of her fairy-tale novels with a twist is *The Two Princesses of Bamarre*, in which a brave sister falls ill with the Gray Death. Her timid sister must overcome her fears to confront four monsters in a quest to save her.

Levine departed from her usual fairy-tale plots and made her own family her inspiration in *Dave at Night*. This book is loosely based on her father's experiences while growing up in the Hebrew Orphan Asylum in New York City. In a Dickensian story, Dave leads a double life, sneaking out of the orphanage at night into the **jazz** world of **Harlem** in 1926. Levine combined her own personal experiences with a fairy-tale theme in *The Wish*. She had a bad year in

Commercial Art

Commercial art refers to art that is used in promoting business. It utilizes a variety of creative techniques, among them photography, illustration, music, video, television commercials, computer-generated imagery, and graphic design.

p.405

Jazz

In New Orleans, Louisiana, around 1900, a new genre of music was born which was characterized by prominent meter, improvisation, distinctive tone colors and performance techniques, and syncopated rhythmic patterns. This unique style of music, which draws on the African American experience and human emotion as a source of inspiration, is called jazz. Jazz musicians generally perform on horn, saxophone, piano, and percussion instruments. It is hard to define jazz as there are many different styles of music that are influenced by jazz, including Dixieland, Swing, Bebop, and the Blues.

JAMES MOODY STAGE

the tenth grade and uses that experience in this novel about an unpopular eighth-grader. Unlike Levine, however, her heroine has the help of magic in gaining popularity, as she is granted a wish in return for a kindness.

— Lisa Rowe Fraustino

Sonia Levitin

Born: August 18, 1934; Berlin, Germany

www.bol.ucla.edu/~slevitin/index.html

Sonia Levitin has written a broad spectrum of literature for children and young adults, including picture books, **historical novels**, murder mysteries, and humorous stories. She has used her own childhood memories extensively in her work, and is particularly interested in Jewish history and themes. Her fiction underlines the commonality of human emotions and psychology throughout history and cultures and deals particularly with themes of independence and freedom.

p.1

Levitin was born in Germany, but her family fled the Nazis when she was four years old, leaving most of their money and possessions behind. The family then settled in Los Angeles, California, where they struggled to establish themselves. Sonia eventually attended the University of California at Berkeley, where she met her husband. After the birth of her first child she became serious about writing. She wrote a newspaper column and taught creative writing but it was her decision to write about her family's history that launched her long and successful career.

In *Journey to America*, *Silver Days*, and *Annie's Promise*, Levitin creates a fictionalized version of her family history. *Journey to America* chronicles their escape from **Nazi Germany** in the 1930's, *Silver Days* deals with the difficulties of adjusting to a

p.40

totally new way of life in a new country, and *Annie's Promise* continues to treat the difficulties of growing up caught between two cultures.

Levitin's historical novel *Escape from Egypt* is a coming-of-age story set during the biblical time of the Israelites' Exodus from Egypt. Its protagonist p.233 is a Hebrew slave named Jesse who falls in love with Jennat, a half-Egyptian, half-Syrian girl. The story involves their adventures during the Exodus and their adjustment to their newfound freedom. Through strong characterizations Levitin brings new life to this familiar biblical tale and offers a deeper understanding of historical and spiritual issues.

The Cure combines Levitin's interest in Jewish history with science fiction. Sixteen-year-old Gemm is banished from the world of the year 2047 because he has expressed an interest in music, a banned

Nazi Germany

On January 30, 1933, Adolf Hitler took the oath of office, which made him chancellor of the German Republic. In the following weeks, Hitler persuaded President Paul von Hindenburg to use his constitutional authority to prohibit political opposition and suspend civil rights. By July 1933, the Communists and Social Democrats had been suppressed and by July 14, the National Socialist (Nazi) Party was declared the only party in Germany. Under the rule of Hitler, the Nazis final goal was not simply to harass the Jews but actually to annihilate them. In the end, other nations closed their eyes to the atrocities, and many of them even refused to allow Jews to immigrate. The White Paper issued by Great Britain in 1939 severely restricted immigration to Palestine and, in effect, shut off Jewish escape from Europe. On January 30, 1939, Hitler predicted that Europe's Jews would be destroyed. Before World War II was over, the Nazis would succeed in killing more than six million Jewish people, a tragedy later known as the Holocaust.

Sydney Taylor Award

The Sydney Taylor Award is given annually to two books, one for younger readers and one for older readers, which exemplify a significant contribution to Jewish literature. It was first established by Ralph Taylor in memory of his wife, the author of the "All-of-a-Kind Family" book series, Sydney Taylor. The Association of Jewish Libraries (AJL) chose to recognize Sydney Taylor for her unique contribution to Jewish literature by portraying Jewish life in a way that was both authentic and enjoyable. Therefore, the first Sydney Taylor Award was awarded in her honor in 1968 and continues to be given periodically.

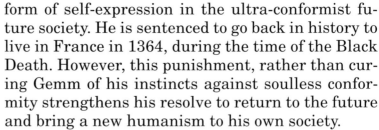

form of self-expression in the ultra-conformist future society. He is sentenced to go back in history to live in France in 1364, during the time of the Black Death. However, this punishment, rather than curing Gemm of his instincts against soulless conformity strengthens his resolve to return to the future and bring a new humanism to his own society.

Incident at Loring Groves, based on a true story, takes place in a contemporary suburban setting. When a group of partying teenagers breaks into a cottage and then discovers the body of a murdered girl, they make a pact to tell no one of their discovery, fearing that the revelation may damage their reputations and future college plans. Two members struggle with the conflict between peer pressure and their own developing moral values.

p.408

Sonia Levitin received the **Sydney Taylor Award** for distinguished contribution to Jewish Children's Literature and the **Edgar Allan Poe Award** in the juvenile category for *Incident at Loring Groves*. In 1981 she was awarded by the **Southern California Council on Literature for Children and Young People** for her entire body of work.

p.7

– Mary Virginia Davis

C. S. Lewis

Born: November 29, 1898; Belfast, Northern Ireland
Died: November 22, 1963; Oxford, England

www.cslewis.org

p.173

p.104

p.87

680

p.32

C. S. Lewis and his Oxford University colleague **J. R. R. Tolkien** are credited with reviving the fantasy genre in the middle of the twentieth century. The writing of pure fantasy—stories set in completely imaginary worlds—had faded before the glamour of hard science fiction. Lewis and Tolkien had formed a club called the Inklings, who critiqued each other's writings. Unable to find the kind of novels that they wanted to read, the two challenged each other to write their own. Tolkien was to write a time-travel story and Lewis a space-travel story, both with the aim of bringing myth back into fiction. Tolkien's story eventually petered out; Lewis's turned into *Out of the Silent Planet*.

Lewis was born into a **middle-class** family in Belfast. His father was a lawyer, and his mother, a vivacious woman to whom Lewis was very close, died when he was nine. He had an older brother, Warren, who was to remain one of his closest companions throughout his life. Lewis's school experiences were traumatic. After the headmaster at his first school was removed and put in a mental hospital, Lewis was educated by a tutor, William Kirkpatrick, from whom he learned a rigorous intellectual style which led to atheism. After serving in the British army during World War I, Lewis returned to Oxford to complete his education and eventually became a fellow of Magdalen College, Oxford. As a scholar of medieval and Renaissance literature, how-

TITLES

The Space trilogy:

Out of the Silent Planet, 1938

Perelandra, 1943

That Hideous Strength, 1945

The Chronicles of Narnia:

The Lion, the Witch, and the Wardrobe, 1950

Prince Caspian, 1951

The Voyage of the Dawn Treader, 1952

The Silver Chair, 1953

The Horse and His Boy, 1954

The Magician's Nephew, 1955

The Last Battle, 1956

ever, he found himself wondering why the writers whom he most respected were Christians, yet he was not. Tolkien was instrumental in convincing Lewis of the philosophical truth of Christianity, and Lewis went on to make his name as a **Christian apologist**, a theme that underlies his fiction as well as his nonfiction writing.

p.410

Lewis's Space trilogy, *Out of the Silent Planet*, *Perelandra*, and *That Hideous Strength*, presents a very Christian battle between Good and Evil in the context of travel among Earth, Mars, and Venus. His hero, philologist Dr. Elwin Ransom (a character based in part on Tolkien), battles the machinations of the evil Dr. Weston, who is intent on exploiting the resources of the other planets as imperialist European countries had exploited Asia and Africa. Indeed, Weston regards the inhabitants of Mars and Venus in much the same way that Victorian explorers of the earth regarded the "savages" they encountered.

Lewis's best-known works of fantasy, however, p.8 take place in his alternate world of Narnia. The Narnia books were Lewis's attempt to write the kind of story he had enjoyed reading as a child, full of magic and adventure and populated by beings from classical mythology—such as fauns, centaurs, and dryads—and folktales, such as talking animals. Narnia was created by and is watched over

Christian apologist

The term "apologetics" is used to refer to the study of the defense of a doctrine or belief. Christian apologists attempt to show that the Christian faith is not irrational, that believing in it is not against human reason, and that, in fact, Christianity contains values and promotes ways of life more in accord with human nature than other faiths or beliefs. C. S. Lewis was one of the most prolific Christian apologists of the twentieth century.

The Crusades

Fought between 1096 and 1464, the Crusades, or "Wars of the Cross," were a defining feature of the High Middle Ages in Europe. For almost four centuries, between nine and ten major military expeditions left the West for the Middle East in an effort to achieve two strategic goals. One was to prevent the conquest of the Byzantine Empire, a Christian stronghold, by the Muslim Turks. The other goal, which was more important to the Europeans, was to establish Christian control over the pilgrimage sites in the Holy Land, especially Jerusalem. Ultimately, neither aim was permanently secured. The Turks conquered Constantinople in 1453, ending forever the Byzantine Empire. By 1515, all the East, including Palestine, fell under the control of the Turks. The Crusades, however, represent the West's earliest effort to expand and create what rightly has been called "Europe's first adventure in colonialism."

by the very Christ-like figure of Aslan the Lion. Except for *The Horse and His Boy*, all the Narnia books tell of Narnian adventures of people of this world—mostly the Penvensie family of Peter, Susan, Edmund, and Lucy, and their friends. Narnia is opposed by the **totalitarian** land of Calormen to its south; the two countries are very much based on the opposition between Christians and Muslims during Earth's medieval **Crusades**. p.411 Lewis tosses in some Irish mythology as well–*The Voyage of the Dawn Treader* is based on the Irish legend of the voyage of Saint Brendan. The last two novels, *The Magician's Nephew* and *The Last Battle*, tell the stories of the creation and destruction of the world of Narnia. In the latter, especially, Lewis's Christian agenda almost overwhelms the plot of the story. *The Last Battle* was honored with Britain's **Carnegie Medal**.

Lewis was a renowned and controversial writer and scholar, but ironically, his death on November 22, 1963 was overshadowed by the assassination on that same day of U.S. president John F. Kennedy.

– Leslie Ellen Jones

Astrid Lindgren

Born: November 14, 1907; Vimmerby, Smaaland, Sweden
Died: January 28, 2002; Stockholm, Sweden
www.astridlindgren.se/eng/index_1024.htm

In Pippi Longstocking, **Astrid Lindgren** created one of the most enduring and most eccentric characters in juvenile fiction. Pippi has been loved for sixty years because she speaks to the desire to break free from restrictive social conventions and thumb one's nose at authority.

Lindgren was born on a farm in southern Sweden. Her childhood was spent among farmers, farm hands, and other rural folks, an environment that she recalled as happy and warm, and in which everyone spoke their minds. At the age of nineteen, she went to Stockholm to work as a secretary. Five years later she got married and eventually had two children of her own. Like so many parents, she entertained her children with stories of her own childhood. One day, her daughter was sick and demanded that her mother tell a story about a little girl called "Pippi Longstocking"—a name she made up on the spur of the moment.

Lindgren then began making up stories about a mischievous, red-haired dynamo with enormous strength and no parents around to repress her. Pippi's father was a sea captain who was usually at sea, and her mother was dead. These stories remained within the family until Lindgren broke her ankle several years later and entertained herself during her recovery by writing them down. After her manuscript was rejected by one publisher, Lindgren won second place in a writing contest with another story. A year later, she won first prize with her Pippi story. From then on, Lindgren was a writer.

p.413

p.620

Pippi was Lindgren's most popular character. Lindgren also wrote about mystery-solver Bill Bergson, Emil, a misadventure-prone five-year-old, and many other characters. The constant throughout her writing is the exuberant high spirits of her characters. Pippi, for example, is eccentric, but never mean or destructive. She simply exposes the absurdity of mindless adherence to rules. Tommy and Annika, the two well-behaved children who live next door to her, are shocked yet thrilled by Pippi's escapades. She is a fantasy figure of a child who pleases herself without adults telling her what to do. When her father, Captain Longstock-

Stockholm

Stockholm is the capital and largest city of Sweden. It is located on the eastern coast of Sweden and has a population of about 800,000. It was founded in the late twelfth century and became one of the most important centers in northern Europe. The old section of the city, Gamla Stan, has been the seat of power for the Swedish Kingdom for centuries.

ing, is around, he does not try to repress his daughter either.

Pippi has many traits in common with folktale characters, such as her superhuman strength (she can lift her horse over her head and beats a circus strongman in a fight). She is, in fact, an example of the **trickster** figure of folklore and mythology, a type of character found worldwide who disrupts conventional society, trails chaos in his or her wake, and generally shakes things up. Tricksters such as Pippi—and many of Lindgren's other characters, such as Emil and Mischievous Meg—are humorous figures who remind people of the importance of not taking themselves too seriously.

In 1958 Astrid Lindgren received Denmark's **Hans Christian Andersen Medal** for her entire body of work.

– Leslie Ellen Jones

Trickster character in literature

The definition of a Trickster varies due to the many roles that he or she plays. For example, a Trickster may either be callous or loveable, selfish or a hero, clever or foolish. Many times when the Trickster is portrayed as foolish, he takes on a humorous role as well. Much of the humor stems from the things the Trickster does that are wrong or when she or he acts in a stupid or foolish manner. Native American literature casts the coyote as the Trickster. The Trickster serves an important role in literature, many times as an outlet for strong emotion or actions.

Eric Linklater

Born: March 8, 1899; Penarth, Wales
Died: November 7, 1974; Aberdeen, Scotland
www.kirjasto.sci.fi/linklate.htm

p.42

Eric Linklater initially improvised the rambling tale told in *The Wind on the Moon* to amuse two children, and was surprised when the book won Great Britain's **Carnegie Medal**. The story was created during the height of World War II, and at that time Linklater was working in the public relations department of the War Office. The breezy frivolity of the early chapters of *The Wind on the Moon* must have been a welcome relief from his work as a wartime propagandist, which included writing a series of morale-building **plays for radio** broadcasting. He had previously served as an officer in the Royal Engineers and had also fought in World War I as a private in the Black Watch. It is thus not surprising that the latter chapters of both *The Wind on the Moon* and *The Pirates in the Deep Green Sea* evolve into quirky celebrations of British military opposition to would-be dictators.

The Wind on the Moon features two sisters, Dinah and Dorinda, whose well-intentioned attempts to be good frequently go awry. In the first half of the novel the local witch, Mrs. Grimble, supplies them with a potion with which they transform themselves into animals. With the potion's aid they take up residence in the local zoo and solve the mystery of the ostrich's stolen eggs. In the second half they journey to Europe to rescue their father, Major Palfrey, who has been imprisoned by the arrogant dictator of the fictional Bombardy, Count Hulagu Bloot. They are aided in this quest by two veteran military engineers ("sappers") who have been tunnelling since

p.564

TITLES

The Wind on the Moon, 1944

The Pirates in the Deep Green Sea, 1949

Crimean War (1853-1856)

The Crimean War, fought by Britain, France, and the Ottoman Turks against Russia, took place in an era during which the major European powers sought to build their empires. Russia had long coveted access to the Mediterranean Sea through the Straits of the Dardanelles and the Bosporus, both of which remained in Turkish hands in the 1850's. Russia, France, and Britian were competing for trade with the Ottoman Empire, and Russian expansion into the Mediterranean could threaten their interests as well as the territorial integrity of the Ottoman Empire itself. Therefore, at the end of March 1854, Britain and France declared war on Russia. The major military goal of the Allied forces was to invade the Crimean Peninsula and eventually to capture the Russian naval base at Sevastopol. Once that fortress finally fell in 1855, the war's major fighting ended and peace negotiations soon began.

the **Crimean War** of 1854. In parallel with these principal plot threads is a wealth of amiably nonsensical material, including a good deal of comic verse, which carries forward the great tradition of British colleagues **Edward Lear** and Lewis Carroll (author of *Alice's Adventures in Wonderland*).

p.410

p.417

Although *The Pirates in the Deep Green Sea* seems slightly contrived in comparison with its predecessor, it is equally uninhibited and eminently readable. Two brothers, Timothy and Hew, are enabled to breathe underwater by a magic oil given to them by the long-lived Gunner Boles, whose character recalls the sappers of the earlier novel. Boles and the intelligent octopus Cully share the duty of guarding one of the knots that tie Earth's lines of latitude and longitude together to secure a grid holding the continents in place. When the knot is threatened by the evil pirates Inky Poops and Dan Scumbril, Timothy and Hew seek help from the legendary Davy Jones and his ragtag army of former naval officers, which includes a good many so-called pirates. The fact that the pseudonymous Jones's motto is *Floreat Etona* ("may Eton prosper") links him to Captain Hook in James M. Barrie's *Peter Pan*. He is as proud of having been taught by Nicholas Udall—the "flogging headmaster" of **Eton** who went on to become a pre-Shakespearean court playwright after being dismissed—as he is of having sailed around the world with Sir Francis Drake.

p.200

Eric Linklater's satirical account of an innocent abroad in the United States, *Juan in America* (1930), might also be of interest to young adult readers.

– Brian Stableford

Edward Lear

Edward Lear, born in 1812, is known primarily for his absurd wit and "nonsense poetry." Although he began his career as an artist, he is remembered today for his humor and his timeless contribution to literature. The subject and form of many of his works vary greatly, however, all can be characterized by his irreverent view of the world. Lear liked to poke fun at everything, including himself. He used this method to especially deal with the strict and sometimes lifeless Victorian society. His favorite poetic style was the limerick, a comic five-line poem with a set rhyme pattern and line lengths, helping to make the verse sound silly.

Robert Lipsyte

Born: January 16, 1938; New York, New York

www.education.wisc.edu/ccbc/lipsyte.htm

Robert Lipsyte's novels are concerned with boys coming of age and overcoming problems through determination and positive values. His characters deal with issues such as body image, anger, drugs, bullies and other challenges that face adolescents. The theme of overcoming adversity running through Lipsyte's novels reflects situations in his own life. Overweight until the age of fourteen, he spent much of his time alone reading and writing. He decided to become a writer because it would allow him to hide behind his typewriter.

When Lipsyte graduated from Columbia University, he planned to attend graduate school but ended up working as a copy boy for *The New York Times* sports department. Over the next fourteen years he worked his way up to writing a weekly sports column that eventually became internationally syndicated. His experience covering boxing led to the idea for his first novel for young people, *The Contender*, in 1967. By 1971 he had retired from journalism and he was devoting all of his time to writing novels.

In 1978 Lipsyte was diagnosed with cancer. He stopped writing to concentrate on getting well. After undergoing successful chemotherapy he was able to get back to writing. Since then he has written books for adults and adolescents, and scripts for movies and television. His writing career came full circle in 1991, when he once again began writing a weekly sports column for *The New York Times*.

p.419

Chemotherapy

The term "chemotherapy" refers to the use of chemical agents in the treatment of any disease. Most often it applies to the treatment of cancer. Some drugs are capable either of stopping the spread of cancer cells or preventing cancer from occurring at all. These drugs, called chemotherapeutic agents, destroy cells. Chemotherapy is used when cancerous cells have spread throughout the body and their location cannot be precisely determined. Neither surgery nor radiation therapy can destroy widespread cancer, but drugs can circulate throughout the entire body and kill the cells that surgery and radiotherapy miss. There are several different types of chemotherapeutic agents that are used, including alkylating agents, antimetabolites, antitumor antibiotics, vinka alkaloids, hormonal therapy, and platinum analogues.

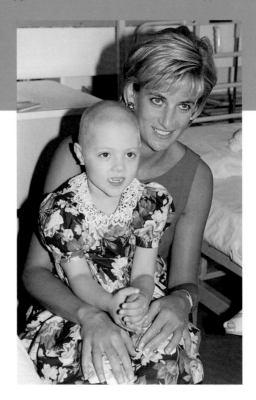

p.233
p.296

Alfred Brooks, the young African American **protagonist** in *The Contender*, seems to have no future. He lives in **Harlem**, has dropped out of high school, and can find only menial jobs. One day he finds himself in a gym and begins to learn the discipline and skills needed to become a boxer. *The Brave* is a sequel to *The Contender* in which Alfred is now a New York City policeman. He meets Sonny Bear, a young, angry Native American boxer who has become entangled in the New York City underworld. Brooks sets Sonny Bear up to train at the same gym that turned his life around, but Sonny must decide for himself between the discipline and hard work of boxing and the attraction of street life.

In *The Chemo Kid*, Lipsyte draws on his own experiences with cancer to create the character of Fred, a sixteen-year-old who has been diagnosed with cancer. Fred is undergoing experimental chemotherapy and this may explain the sudden appearance of superhuman powers that allow him to combat crime

Children's Book Award

The Children's Book Award, known as the Josette Frank Award since 1998, is given to a book of outstanding literary merit in which children or young people deal positively with difficulties and grow emotionally and morally as a result. The winner is selected by the Child Study Committee of the Child Study Association of America. The award is given by New York City's Bank Street College, a leader in child-centered education.

and corporate polluters. In *One Fat Summer*, Lipsyte also uses his experience as an overweight teenager in the character of Bobby Marks. On vacation with his family, fourteen-year-old Bobby learns to stand up for himself. This is the first book in a trilogy that includes *Summer Rules* and *The Summerboy* and follows Bobby as he matures and learns to overcome problems over the course of three summers.

Among the writing honors Robert Lipsyte has received is the 1999 **ALAN Award** for contributions p.16 to Young Adult Literature. *The Contender* won the **Children's Book Award** at Bank Street College.

p.420

– Deborah DePiero

Janet Taylor Lisle

Born: February 13, 1947; Englewood, New Jersey
www.janettaylorlisle.com/index2.htm

p.117

A writer of fables, fantasies, allegories, and **historical fiction**, **Janet Taylor Lisle** often lifts the curtain between the real and the imagined, giving her readers a peek at the supernatural forces at work on the other side. She says that she believes in the unknown and thinks of magic as being a part of the world that is still waiting to be discovered.

422

Lisle grew up in Connecticut and Rhode Island, whose towns and villages she later used as settings for her tales. She worked as a **VISTA** volunteer for two years and as a journalist for a decade. Her experiences led her to be as comfortable writing about real-world conflicts as she is with fantasy. In *Sirens and Spies*, for example, fourteen-year-old Elsie Potter discovers a shameful secret about her violin teacher, Renee Fitch. Elsie is so repulsed by the secret that she refuses to visit Miss Fitch in the hospital, where the teacher is recovering from a brutal attack. Elsie's sister Mary takes a more liberal view, however, and while the full story of Miss Fitch's past unfolds, the girls learn a lesson in forgiveness and redemption.

In *The Art of Keeping Cool*, set in World War II, a New England boy, Robert, comes face to face with the largest and most powerful long-range weapons of the time. While struggling to unravel the mystery of his fa-

TITLES

Sirens and Spies, 1985

The Great Dimpole Oak, 1987

The Lampfish of Twill, 1991

Forest, 1993

The Art of Keeping Cool, 2000

Crying Rocks, 2003

ther's estrangement from his own domineering father, Robert and his cousin Eliot make friends with a painter suspected of being a German spy. The boys must prevail against the hatred and betrayal of the community during a tense time of war.

The undiscovered magic of *The Lampfish of Twill* lies under the sea. This book tells of an orphan boy, Eric, who lives with a stern and emotionally distant aunt. His only real friend is a pet sea gull. Determined to net a giant lampfish, much prized for its bones and meat, Erik befriends a deranged, old fisherman who leads him to a magical world beneath the waves, where motion stops and time stands still. The images are stark and surreal. The theme is that truth is not an absolute; it depends on the viewpoint of the truth seeker.

Lisle is fond of animals and often converses with them, believing that humans do not possess the only languages in the world. Communication and social structure among animals play an important part in *Forest*. Twelve-year-old Amber unwittingly invades the kingdom of the squirrels and nearly triggers a war. However, she manages to avoid violence through some bold diplomacy. Lisle's love of natural history shows in the details of squirrel life she weaves into

VISTA Program

For more than thirty five years the Corporation for National Service has run a full-time, year-long program called the AmeriCorps Volunteers In Service To America (VISTA). VISTA is open to men and women eighteen years and older from all backgrounds. Through VISTA, thousands of men and women are sent to work with an approved public or nonprofit sponsoring organization at one of nine hundred sites in high-need areas across the country. VISTA aims to fight illiteracy, improve health services, create businesses, and increase housing opportunities by helping to establish services in low-income communities. Members of VISTA receive a living allowance, education award, and other benefits such as health insurance, training, travel expenses, and student loan deferral.

Rebecca Caudill Young Readers Book Award

The Rebecca Caudill Young Readers Book Award is awarded annually in Illinois for exceptional contributions in children's literature. The award was named for author Rebecca Caudill, who lived and wrote in Urbana, Illinois, for nearly fifty years. It was developed to help encourage children and young adults to read for personal satisfaction. Therefore, children grades 4 though 8 participate in this award by voting for their favorite choice from a list of twenty books. The votes from public schools all over Illinois are tallied to finally determine the winner. Any work nominated for this award must fit the following criteria: have literary merit; be of interest and appeal to children in grades 4 through 8; be copyrighted within the last five years; still be in print at the time of selection; be nonfiction, fiction, or poetry; and the author must be living at the time of nomination and selection to the master list. The Illinois Reading Council, the Illinois School Library Media Association, and the Illinois Association of Teachers of English sponsor the award.

the story. Her respect for all living things is apparent, too, in *The Great Dimpole Oak*. In that fable, two boys who are at odds with a bully join forces with a town matriarch, an Indian swami, and a landowner to save a historic tree.

Janet Taylor Lisle has won wide recognition for her work. *Sirens and Spies*, *The Lampfish of Twill*, and *Forest* were among the **Best Books of the Year** named by the *School Library Journal*. *The Art of Keeping Cool* won the Scott O'Dell Award for Historical Fiction and was nominated for the Rebecca Caudill Young Readers Book Award. *The Great Dimpole Oak* was a Golden Kite Honor Book.

p.195
p.51
p.423
p.111

– Faith Hickman Brynie

Penelope Lively

Born: March 17, 1933; Cairo, Egypt

penelopelively.net

All of award-winning author **Penelope Lively**'s works focus on the presence of the past. The only real difference between the novels she writes for children and young adults and those she writes for adults is that her younger protagonists have fantastic adventures that take them into the historical past, while her adults relive the past in their own memories.

p.23

In her autobiographical book *Oleander Jacaranda: A Childhood Perceived* (1994), Lively recaptures the magic of her childhood in Egypt, where she was born Penelope Margaret Low. She was the only child of Roger Low, a bank manager, and his wife, Vera. With the English nanny who actually reared her, Lively ventured around the ancient cities of Cairo and Alexandria and developed an interest in history. She had few formal lessons; instead, she and her nanny read widely.

p.425

When Penelope was twelve years old, her parents divorced, her beloved nanny was dismissed, and she was sent to a **boarding school** in England, where sports were valued above academics. After three miserable years, she entered St. Anne's College of Oxford University, where she earned a bachelor's degree in modern history in 1954. Three years later she married Jack Lively, who became a professor of political theory.

p.1€

p.173

Penelope Lively so enjoyed reading to her two young children that she decided to try writing children's fiction. Her first published book, *Astercote* (1970) is the story of a chalice that villagers believed could protect them from evil. Her later works typically intertwine the past and the present.

Lively's first book to feature a young adult protagonist was *The House in Norham Gardens*. Its fourteen-year-old heroine, Clare Mayfield, lives with her great-aunts in a Victorian mansion in North Oxford. On the walls are artifacts brought back from New Guinea by Clare's great-grandfather, an anthropologist. After finding a sacred ceremonial shield in the attic, Clare begins visiting her great-grandfather's New Guinea in dreams so vivid that she begins confusing them with reality.

In *A Stitch in Time*, eleven-year-old Maria Foster has a similar experience. Maria's parents rent a Victorian house for the summer. In the old house she finds a century-old **sampler** that was sewn by a girl her own age. It makes her so intensely aware of the past that she hears ghostly noises and feels herself strangely linked with that earlier era. Like Clare,

Alexandria, Egypt

Founded by Macedonian king Alexander the Great in 332-331 B.C., Alexandria stands today as the second largest city and main port of Egypt. Built by architect Dinocrates on order of the ruler, the city quickly flourished into a prominent intellectual, political, and economic metropolis. With beautiful white sand beaches and magnificent scenery, Alexandria is located northwest of the Nile River delta and stretches along a narrow strip between the Mediterranean Sea and Lake Mariut.

Maria must learn how to live in the present while recognizing the inescapable presence of the past.

In their intellectual and psychological subtlety, these two novels are precursors to Lively's later books for adults. However, they owe their popularity among young adults to the fact that, just as with her books for children, her readers find it so easy to identify with her daring, imaginative, and thoroughly likeable protagonists.

Penelope Lively has the unusual distinction of winning both the **Whitbread Award** for children's fiction and a **Booker-McConnell Prize** for her adult novel *Moon Tiger* (1987). *The House in Norham Gardens* was an American Library Association **Notable Book**, and both of Lively's young adult novels were *Horn Book Magazine* **Honor Books**. In 1976 *A Stitch in Time* won the prestigious **Whitbread Children's Book of the Year** award.

p.4

— Rosemary M. Canfield Reisman

Sampler

During the eighteenth and nineteenth centuries, many young women went to school to learn how to do needlework. At the end of their course, they completed a sampler, a piece of cloth embroidered with many examples of different stitches. Some samplers are decorated with the alphabet, numbers, flowers, and other decorative images. The sampler was framed and hung in the house. In the mid-1800's, women began gaining access to academic education instead of only learning domestic skills, and samplers became less popular. Today, they have become collectible. At auction, one sampler recently brought a price of $145,500.

Jack London

Born: January 12, 1876; San Francisco, California
Died: November 22, 1916; Glen Ellen, California

sunsite.berkeley.edu/London

Jack London was the **best-selling**, highest paid, and most popular American author of his time. His adventure stories, noted for their realistic settings and compelling characters, dramatize the themes of battling to survive with dignity, maintaining one's individuality, a **Darwinian** view of nature that requires survival of the fittest, and finding love in a world full of cruelty. *White Fang* and *The Call of the Wild*, his famous dog novels, which show the brutality of men toward animals, are both thrilling and ruthless.

Born as John Griffith Chaney, London grew up in the San Francisco Bay Area. He was raised by his mother after his father abandoned the family, and he grew up in poverty. He took his name from his stepfather, John London. The first half of his life was hard, and he had to work at such jobs as coal shoveler, factory worker, and janitor. So it is not surprising that his stories portray life as a struggle. He would later write a highly autobiographical novel of his youth, which he published as *Martin Eden*. At the age of seventeen, London became a sailor, and gained some renown as an oyster pirate, a gold prospector, a war correspondent, a rancher, and even a candidate for mayor of Oakland, California. After he started publishing regularly, he became a celebrity because he was fun-loving, handsome, and adventurous. He was married twice, first to Bessie Maddern, the mother of his two daughters, and then to Charmian Kittredge, the great love of his life.

The Call of the Wild tells the story of Buck, an

.384

.428

TITLES

The Cruise of the Dazzler, 1902

A Daughter of the Snows, 1902

The Call of the Wild, 1903

The Sea-Wolf, 1904

White Fang, 1906

The Game, 1905

Before Adam, 1907

Martin Eden, 1908

Lost Face, 1910

The Mutiny of the Elsinore, 1914

The Scarlet Plague, 1915

Jerry of the Islands, 1917

Michael, Brother of Jerry, 1917

Charles Darwin

Charles Darwin has had an immeasureable influence on the development of modern biology, ecology, morphology, embryology, and paleontology. His theory of evolution established a natural history of the earth and enabled humans to see themselves for the first time as part of the natural order of life. While they may disagree about details, most modern biologists agree that evolutionary theory remains the only viable scientific explanation for the diversity of life on earth.

intelligent dog who lives on a California estate belonging to a kind judge. However, after the embittered gardener sells Buck, he becomes a sled dog in Alaska, and his life changes dramatically. Buck p.42 learns to fear humans with their whips and clubs, to be wary of the vicious lead-dog Spitz, and to work hard with insufficient food and rest. Buck becomes a great sled dog and earns the position of lead-dog, but when new masters mistreat him, he is saved from starvation and fatal beatings by the gold prospector John Thornton, with whom he becomes great friends. Eventually, however, Buck is torn between his love for Thornton and the howls of wolves tempting him to leave the world of men and plunge into the wilderness. Buck makes his decision after Thornton is murdered by members of a tribe of Indians. He avenges his master's death by killing as many of the men as possible, then heads into the wild to join up with a friendly band of wolves—his ties with humanity broken forever.

The Call of the Wild was so successful that London decided to write a companion novel, this time on the reverse theme: about a wild dog who becomes civilized. In *White Fang*, the puppy who is three-quarters wolf and one-quarter husky is also forced into work as a sled dog. White Fang is treated cruelly by nearly every man he meets, particularly the ironically named Beauty Smith, and becomes a vicious fighter. He is saved from near death in a caged dog fight by a man named Scott, who takes him back to his cabin and teaches him love and loyalty. Scott brings White Fang to live in a beautiful California valley, but his adventures are not over yet.

Readers love how London tells stories from the point of view of the animals. He describes how they learn to hunt, survive, and fight back against cruelty. London passionately depicts the horrors of **animal abuse**, but he also reveals his great love of life and the beauty of nature itself.

— Fiona Kelleghan

Iditarod Trail Dog Sled Race

In 1925, the remote town of Nome, Alaska, was threatened by a diptheria epidemic. The serum needed to fight the disease was rushed there by dog teams, the first of which was led by the famous Balto, a Siberian husky. This historic event is commemorated with the Iditarod Trail Dog Sled Race.

A tradition begun on March 3, 1973, the Iditarod Trail Dog Sled Race is now known as "the last great race on earth." Beginning in Anchorage, Alaska, and ending 1,100 miles later in Nome, the Iditarod is not only a test of athletic ability, but also a test of courage and endurance. Riders, called mushers, put together a team of dogs and complete a course that stretches over treacherous terrain. The winner of the Iditarod not only wins a cash reward but also achieves a personal victory.

Lois Lowry

Born: March 20, 1937; Honolulu, Hawaii

www.loislowry.com

Lois Lowry's fiction is generally concerned with topics as controversial as mental illness, cancer, and the Jewish **Holocaust**. However, one of her best-known series is lighthearted. Her books usually stress her favorite theme: the importance of human connections. The death of her son, an air force pilot, and her daughter's physical **disability** have given her an awareness of the importance of ending conflict and promoting human understanding—both themes that she emphasizes in her novels.

Born in Hawaii, Lowry grew up the daughter of an army dentist who moved his family all over the world. She attended **Brown University** but left during her sophomore year to marry a navy officer, thus continuing her life as a member of a military family. After she and her husband finally settled in Maine and had four children, she returned to school to earn her bachelor's degree at the University of Southern Maine and finally began the writing career that she had dreamed of since her childhood.

Her first book, *A Summer to Die*, was inspired by the early death of her sister and its effect on the family. In it, thirteen-year-old Meg, who always envied her sister, must cope with her sister's illness and death and the conflicting emotions that she consequently experiences. *Rabble Starkey* also considers a serious theme, this time mental illness, as twelve-year-old Rabble's mother

p.5

p.3

p.43

Brown University

Brown University was founded in 1764 in Warren, Rhode Island. It is the seventh oldest college in the U.S. Originally called the "Rhode Island College," it was later renamed after Nicholas Brown, Jr, one of the first graduates. In 1770, the university moved to its present location in Providence. In 1891, Brown established a Women's College, which was later named Pembroke. A significant change came to the university when, in 1969, it adopted a new curriculum changing the university's status to an Ivy-League school. Brown became coeducational in 1971 when it merged with Pembroke.

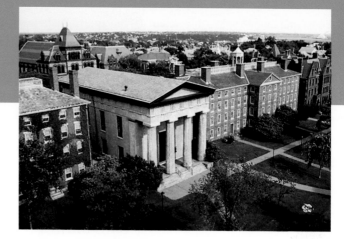

becomes mentally ill, and the Starkeys move in with Rabble's best friend, Veronica Bigelow.

To give herself a break from more serious themes, Lowry created the Anastasia series, beginning with *Anastasia Krupnik*, in which ten-year-old Anastasia falls in love, expects a new baby brother, and gets to know her grandmother. This was followed by *Anastasia Again*, which describes twelve-year-old Anastasia's move from the city to the suburbs. Seven more popular Anastasia books followed these titles.

Number the Stars, in which Lowry returned to more serious themes, is a World War II tale of ten-year-old Annemarie, who helps shelter a Jewish friend from **Nazis in German-occupied Denmark**. She also gets involved in helping smuggle Jews to safety in neutral Sweden. This story is based on the experiences of a friend of Lowry's, who lived through the German occupation of Denmark. Lowry's most controversial book, *The Giver*, is set in a future without war, poverty, fear, or hardship. As twelve-year-old Jonas prepares to receive his life assignment as a "receiver of memory," he discovers the

432

Denmark and Nazi Germany

On April 9, 1940, Nazi Germany invaded Denmark. However, unlike other countries, the people of Denmark were viewed by the Germans as of the same race (the "Aryan" or white "Master race"); therefore, they were not treated as badly as people in other occupied countries. The Nazis saw the benefit of Denmark's resources and left the government in place to function normally. However, before long, the Danes grew tired of German occupation and decided to resist. When the Germans attempted to round up Danish Jews, the Danes had already moved almost all of them to the coast and then to safety in Sweden. Of the approximate five hundred Danish Jews who were sent to camps, about fifty died. In 1945, as Germany fell, the Danes welcomed British troops as liberators.

dark side of his so-called perfect society and sets out on a quest to save the world. The book is thought-provoking and has an uncertain ending that unsettles many readers.

A much-honored author, Lois Lowry received **Newbery Medals** for both *Number the Stars* and *The Giver*. She also received Boston Globe-Horn Book and Golden Kite Awards for *Rabble Starkey*, and an **American Book Award** nomination for *Anastasia Again!*

– Mary Virginia Davis

p.747

Chris Lynch

Born: July 2, 1962; Boston, Massachusetts

www.teenreads.com/authors/au-lynch-chris.asp

Chris Lynch's books are mostly concerned with young men who are separated from their primary communities by aspects of individual character or random chance that mark them as outsiders. Initially distressed or discouraged by their uniqueness, Lynch's **protagonists** must discover and develop inner resources in order to come to terms with forbidding societies or unusual physical or psychological features. Although often grimly realistic, and at times even despairing of the future, Lynch's books are ultimately not pessimistic. In contrast to the dark vision of many of his novels, he has also created an engagingly comic figure, Elvin Bishop, whose journey through adolescence is frequently hilarious despite the difficulties he encounters.

Lynch grew up in a racially mixed blue-collar section of **Boston**. He was drawn more to sports than to studies until he became repelled by the football-factory environment of an all-boys high school he attended. Assuming that he needed to learn a practical skill, he majored in journalism until he took a class in novel writing that helped lead him toward his fiction-writing career. His first book, *Shadow Boxer*, grew out of a class assignment in which he was required to write five pages on an incident in his childhood.

Drawing on his experiences as an adolescent and locating most of his stories in a fictional city similar

TITLES

Shadow Boxer, 1993

Gypsy Davey, 1994

Iceman, 1994

Slot Machine, 1995

Political Timber, 1996

Blue-Eyed Son trilogy:

Mick, 1996

Blood Relations, 1996

Dog Eat Dog, 1996

Extreme Elvin, 1999

Gold Dust, 2000

Freewill, 2001

Who The Man, 2003

The Gravedigger's Cottage, 2004

to Boston, Lynch began writing and publishing steadily during the early 1990's. *Iceman* extended *Shadow Boxer*'s exploration of family tension and sports as an outlet, while *Gypsy Davey* tells the story of a slightly brain-damaged youth who is trying to save his younger sister from a destructive urban environment. Widening his range, Lynch introduced Elvin Bishop in *Slot Machine*, which combines a powerfully satiric critique of a conformist culture with an endearingly amusing and self-reflective protagonist. Lynch continued in this mode in *Political Timber*, a lighthearted and high-spirited account of a teenage boy running for mayor of a small affluent suburb. At the same time he was writing these books, Lynch completed his *Blue-Eyed Son* trilogy, an unsparing examination of racism and violence that is actually one book published in three divisions in response to marketing requirements.

Lynch brought back Elvin Bishop in *Extreme Elvin* which takes his protagonist through a difficult but manageable first year of high school. He then returned to the darker elements of his fundamental social setting in *Freewill* and *Who*

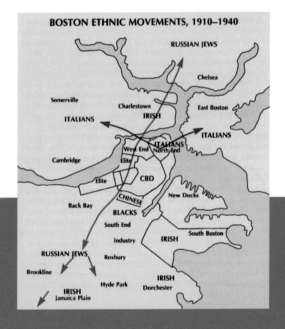

BOSTON ETHNIC MOVEMENTS, 1910–1940

RUSSIAN JEWS

Chelsea

Somerville

Charlestown

East Boston

ITALIANS

IRISH

ITALIANS

West End / North End

ITALIANS

Cambridge

Elite

Elite

CBD

Back Bay

CHINESE

New Docks

BLACKS

South End

Industry

IRISH

South Boston

RUSSIAN JEWS

Roxbury

Brookline

IRISH

Hyde Park

Dorchester

IRISH

Jamaica Plain

Ethnic Boston

Colonial Boston was primarily populated by English Protestants. After 1830 that all changed. Irish Catholics, fleeing famine at home in Ireland, came to Boston in large numbers. Later in the century, immigrants came to Boston from Eastern and Southern Europe. By 1920, immigrants and their children made up 73% of Boston's population. After a period of decreased immigration enforced by government policies, the borders opened once again. This time, immigrants came from Asia, the Caribbean, Latin America, and Africa. By the end of the 1990's, less than half of Boston's residents were white.

Woodcarving

Woodcarving is specifically the art of shaping statues, ornaments, furniture and utensils out of wood by using cutting tools, drills, and abrasives to create, restore, or repair useful or decorative objects. Different woods offer varied qualities that make them suitable for creating particular types of objects.

the Man. In what might be considered his most penetrating representation of inner turmoil, the narration of *Freewill* is presented from the intense but restricted perspective of a seventeen-year-old boy whose parents die in an automobile accident. Feeling isolated and alone, he focuses on **woodcarving** but becomes further disturbed when pieces of his work are found near the bodies of teenage suicides. *Who the Man* reprises the theme of *Shadow Boxer* as a big, strong boy hides his vulnerability and sensitivity with displays of force. Earl Pryor discovers and learns to rely on strengths beyond the merely physical when the people and institutions on which he depends prove deficient in the things that he really needs.

Chris Lynch received **American Library Association** **Best Books for Young Adults** awards for *Slot Machine*, *Gold Dust*, and *Freewill*, and the latter was also a **Michael L. Printz Honor Book**.

— Leon Lewis

435

p.45

488

p.480

George Ella Lyon

Born: April 25, 1949; Harlan, Kentucky

www.visitingauthors.com/authors/lyon_george_ella/
lyon_george_ella_bio.html

George Ella Lyon's books typically focus on characters who sense or come to discover a kinship with characters of other places and other times. Through imagination and inspiration, her characters can relate to the issues of people who came before them or who live in other lands and thereby can gain insights into their own problems.

Born George Ella Hoskins, Lyon grew up in her native eastern Kentucky listening to stories about family life in the local mountains and surrounding areas. Although she was born with poor eyesight, she actually had an easy transition from listening to stories to reading and writing them. She was most interested in poetry, and, in the second grade, began writing poems—a practice she has continued throughout her life. In 1972 she married Stephen C. Lyon, a musician, and received a master's degree from the University of Arkansas in the same year. During the next eleven years, she earned a doctoral degree in English and creative writing from Indiana University, worked at a variety of jobs, and gave birth to her first son.

After composing a picture book for children, Lyon began to write books for children. Spurred by questions about the world her young son had while he was growing up—and which she had recorded in a journal—she began a series of books in the tradition of the stories she had heard in her youth that imaginatively link children and their families with other families of different places and times. While most of Lyon's books are for young children, she wrote several for older children.

In *Borrowed Children*, a novel set in the Great p.437 Depression, a girl named Amanda is forced to act as mother and housekeeper while her mother is ill. When Amanda takes a holiday, she comes to understand and appreciate her life of drudgery in Kentucky. The .233 protagonist in *Here and Then* participates in a Civil War reenactment and is connected across time as she "becomes" the nurse she plays, going back in time to help her save lives.

Lyon has also written two novels specifically for young adult readers. Both involve leaps of imagination and sympathy that allow their characters to connect with other people and enlarge their under-

The Great Depression

The Stock Market Crash of October 29, 1929 (Black Tuesday) sent the United States into the longest and darkest economic depression of its history. American stocks were suddenly worthless, and, overnight, rich investors were poor. This led to panic and a run on the banks with customers withdrawing all their money. The economic crisis snowballed, and between 1929 and 1933,

the country's wealth plummeted wildly. The gross national product (GNP), the total of all goods and services produced each year, fell from more than $100 billion in 1929 to about $74 billion in 1933. Industrial production declined fifty-one percent before it began to rise slightly in 1932.

standing of themselves and others. *With a Hammer for My Heart* is told through different voices in alternate chapters as each character expresses love, desire or rage in her effort to understand a tormented, homeless man who is beset with demons following his wartime service.

p.732

Lyon expressed her interest in time-travel in *Gina.Jamie.Father.Bear*, whose main character goes on a dreamlike journey and encounters a boy who is also searching for the reason for his father's odd behavior. Each tells his own story in a voice full of symbolism and ambiguity. In seeking to uncover the family's secrets, each discovers a strong love between their parents and themselves.

George Ella Lyon has received various awards for her children's books, including the Golden Kite Award, awarded by the Society of Children's Book Writers for *Borrowed Children*. She also received the Jesse Stuart Media Award for her writings on Kentucky by the Kentucky School Media Association.

p.111

p.438

p.1

– Mary Hurd

Jesse Stuart Media Award

The Jesse Stuart Media Award is awarded by the Kentucky School Media Association, a division of the Kentucky Library Association, for creative work which is considered to have made a contribution to the development of media in Kentucky. It can honor a book, a video, a film, an electronic presentation, or other informative and educational project. This award was created in memory of Jesse Stuart, a teacher for much of his life in Kentucky schools and also a successful and famous Kentucky-born writer known for his tales set in W-Hollow. Stuart was named poet laureate of Kentucky in 1954.

Mary E. Lyons

Born: November 28, 1947; Macon, Georgia

www.lyonsdenbooks.com

Mary E. Lyons was born in Georgia, and her family moved frequently when she was a child. By the time she was eleven, she had lived in eight different towns in five different southern states. She never had chances to form long-lasting friendships in school, but was encouraged to read as much as she liked. Meanwhile, she attended a number of all-white Roman Catholic girls' schools until she was in eleventh grade, when she transferred to a public high school. Even so, her life was confined to the white South until she was in college. At the time of the assassination of civil rights leader Martin Luther King, Jr., in 1968, Lyons was the only white person working in a city employment agency, in which she saw at first hand how unfairly African Americans were treated. As part of an education class she took in college, she tutored a black girl who lived just outside of town limits that had been carefully drawn so as to avoid providing city services to the African Americans who lived in urban areas. After college, she worked as a teacher at an all-black inner city school. Lyons found herself becoming drawn to the marginalized and invisible people of society.

Lyons was a reading teacher for seventeen years, and then got a master's **degree in library science** and became a school **librarian**. She began to notice that while her reading students had enjoyed the African American and Afro-Caribbean folktales collected by **Zora Neale Hurston** in the early twentieth century, there was no biography of Hurston for them to read in the school library, so she

p.134

p.35

.440

TITLES

Raw Head, Bloody Bones: African American Tales of the Supernatural (edited), 1991

Letters from a Slave Girl: The Story of Harriet Jacobs, 1992

The Butter Tree: Tales of Bruh Rabbit, 1995

The Poison Place, 1997

Dear Ellen Bee: A Civil War Scrapbook of Two Union Spies (with Muriel M. Branch), 2000

Knockabeg: A Famine Tale, 2001

Zora Neale Hurston

To Alice Walker, the African American writer who documented her own discovery of Zora Neale Hurston in the collection of feminist *essays In Search of our Mothers' Gardens*, Zora Neale Hurston represented an artistic foremother whose achievements and defiance of conventional roles for women were inspiring. Hurston's efforts to preserve, nurture, and transmit African American folk culture were based on her belief that folklore was the common person's art form and that black folklore provided America with its greatest cultural wealth. Her ability to capture the sounds of folk speech and to retell the imaginative stories of African Americans was the foundation of her talent as a writer of fiction. Living most of her life in obscurity and buried in an unmarked grave, Hurston lived and wrote with a confidence and self acceptance that made her a favorite model for later generations of writers.

wrote *Sorrow's Kitchen: The Life and Folklore of Zora Neale Hurston* (1990). Hurston's folktale collections then inspired her to make a collection of African American folktales, *Raw Head, Bloody Bones*. She later published a collection of tales about the African American **trickster** Brer Rabbit.

Lyons began venturing into fiction with *Letters from a Slave Girl*, based on the true story of Harriet Jacobs, a slave who escaped to the North in 1842 after hiding for seven years in her grandmother's cabin. This book won Lyons a Golden Kite Award. Rather than telling a connected story in the style of an epistolary novel, the letters, based on Jacobs's autobiography, capture moments in her life, providing a window on the experiences of slavery. *The Poison Place* also deals with the effects of slavery, telling the stories of Charles Willson Peale, a white portrait painter, and his former slave, Moses Wil-

p.41

p.11

p.441

liams, who became the first black professional artist in post-Revolutionary America. *Dear Ellen Bee* is presented in the form of a scrapbook kept by a southern woman and her former slave, whom she has emancipated and sent to Philadelphia to be educated. As the Civil War develops, the two scheme to get Liza, the former slave, placed in Confederate president Jefferson Davis's household as a Union spy.

With *Knockabeg*, Lyons turns her attention from the oppression suffered by African Americans to that suffered by the Irish during the great Potato Famine of 1845-1850. The famine, in this tale, has been caused by the Nuckelavees, evil fairies who have cursed the potato vines, and the queen of the Trooping Fairies attempts to quell them by raising a human champion to fight for her.

– Leslie Ellen Jones

Epistolary Novel

The epistolary novel is a novel presented in the form of a series of letters. Its history reaches back to classical literature. It also was popular with European writers of the seventeenth and eighteenth centuries. Samuel Richardson's *Pamela,* Jean-Jacques Rousseau's *The New Héloïse*, and Johann Wolfgang von Goethe's *The Sorrows of Young Werther,* are all well-known novels written in letter form. The form fell out of favor in the nineteenth and early twentieth centuries but was rediscovered late in the twentieth century by avant-garde writers such as John Barth, whose 1979 novel *Letters* uses seven letter-writers' voices.

Anne McCaffrey

Born: April 1, 1926; Cambridge, Massachusetts

www.annemccaffrey.org

Anne McCaffrey is a highly productive writer and one of the first women to write science fiction in the United States. She has written several series, both alone and with coauthors, but her best-known and longest series is the Dragonriders of Pern. McCaffrey's emphasis on emotion and character development, as well as her depiction of strong female protagonists, has led some critics to regard her writing as fantasy or, at best, science fantasy, but McCaffrey is insistent on the science aspect of her fiction. Her dragons, for instance, are not the malevolent lizards of mythology but genetically engineered, symbiotic, telepathic beasts who have been designed to work in tandem with their human counterparts.

McCaffrey's father was an army colonel, and her mother a real estate agent. Her mother encouraged her to look beyond marriage and children to a career.

After a childhood in which McCaffrey spent more time in the company of books and horses than with friends, she attended Radcliffe College, the women's college associated with Harvard University (which at that time was all male), majoring in Slavonic languages and literature. After finishing college she worked as a copywriter and married

p.233

p.8?

p.30

p.443

H. Wright Johnson at the age of twenty-four. She began writing during the time she was at home as a mother and has continued for over thirty years. In the 1990's, McCaffrey began a series of collaborations with other female science-fiction writers, including Elizabeth Moon, Jody Lynn Nye, and Mercedes Lackey. Some of these collaborations led to the development of McCaffrey's earlier stand-alone novels into series.

McCaffrey has created several self-contained fictional universes. Her planet of Pern is an Earth colony so far in the future that its inhabitants have forgotten that Earth ever existed. The Dinosaur Planet series features interplanetary travel, dinosaurs, and the Federation of Sentient Planets. Doona is a planet inhabited by two sets of colonists—humans and the catlike Hrruban—who must learn to coexist. The Ship series posits a world in which the brains of people with severe physical disabilities are implanted into spaceships that can thus interact with the people who fly them—the brawn. The Freedom series begins with an invasion of Earth by aliens who enslave humankind and follows the story of a group of humans and aliens who attempt to create a new, free world.

TITLES

Dinosaur Planet, 1977

Crystal Singer series:

Crystal Singer, 1982

Killashandra, 1985

Crystal Line, 1992

Tower and Hive series:

The Rowan, 1990

Damia, 1991

Damia's Children, 1993

Freedom series:

Freedom's Landing, 1995

Freedom's Choice, 1997

Freedom's Challenge, 1998

Freedom's Ransom, 2002

Telepathy

The term "telepathy" was coined by Frederic W. H. Myers, a French researcher, in 1882, from the Greek *tele* (distant) and *pathe* (feeling). It describes communication from one mind to another without the use of language or the senses. It often is called mind reading. This method of communication was considered acceptable in early societies, but as the scientific method was developed, it came to be tested. Myers founded the Society for Psychical Research in 1884 and the American branch was founded one year later. The earliest experiments placed two people in separate rooms, and then they were told to think of a number. It soon became evident that telepathy is very difficult to test. It remains a much discussed but unproven method of communication today.

p.444

Telepathy is a common thread in many of McCaffrey's novels. The Dragonriders of Pern communicate telepathically with their dragons; the Talents of the Tower and Hive series and the protagonists of the Pegasus series are telepaths as well. The Petaybee series and Dinosaur Planet series allow even planets to have feelings. In part, this motif allows for a rational way of allowing alien races to communicate with one another, but it also evokes desires for perfect communication, mind to mind, with no possibility of misunderstanding, that transcend love. Another overarching theme is that of heroism. In true space-opera form, McCaffrey's protagonists are always confronted with obstacles to their success and their hearts' desires, and they always, eventually, win out.

– Leslie Ellen Jones

Robin McKinley

Born: November 16, 1952; Warren, Ohio

www.robinmckinley.com/index.html

p.87

Robin McKinley is best known for her works of fantasy, especially those involving the imaginary land of Damar. At the center of most of her works are strong female characters who excel in such activities as riding, hunting, and swordplay.

Born in Ohio, McKinley was a member of a military family that moved often. She lived in such diverse places as California, New York, and Japan, and her books draw on strange, exotic places for most of their settings. McKinley has said that she found books more reliable than people as friends. From an early age she wanted to be an author. At 446 **Bowdoin College** in Maine, she majored in English literature.

McKinley's books contain strong, honorable role models for women. Her first book, *Beauty*, is a retelling of the classic Beauty and the Beast fairy tale, p.233 with a strong protagonist who has two loving sisters. *Rose Daughter* is another retelling of the same tale. McKinley's other retellings include *The Outlaws of Sherwood*, her version of the Robin Hood 645 tales, and *Spindle's End*, her version of the Sleeping Beauty legend. In each retelling, McKinley makes the material her own.

p.447

The Blue Sword, *The Hero and the Crown*, and *Deerskin* illustrate the kinds of female hero McKinley creates. In all these stories, the women are self-reliant warriors who fight for what is right. *The Blue Sword*, although published earlier, is set long after *The Hero and the Crown*. In it, Harry Crewe discovers that she must lead the people of the imaginary

TITLES

Beauty: A Retelling of the Story of Beauty and the Beast, 1978

The Blue Sword, 1982

The Hero and the Crown, 1984

The Outlaws of Sherwood, 1988

Deerskin, 1993

Rose Daughter, 1997

Spindle's End, 2000

Bowdoin College

Maine was still a part of Massachusetts when Bowdoin College was founded in 1794 by an act signed by Governor Samuel Adams . In 1820 Maine became a state, and Bowdoin has enjoyed its location in Brunswick, Maine, ever since. Bowdoin had an all-male student body until 1971, when

the first female students began to attend classes. Bowdoin has graduated some noteworthy Americans, among them President Franklin Pierce (1824) and his friend Nathaniel Hawthorne (1825). In 1826, John Brown Russwurm graduated from Bowdoin and became the third African American to graduate from an American college. Today, Bowdoin is a four-year liberal arts college with a prestigious reputation.

land of Damar against their northern enemies. She does so reluctantly with the help of the magical Blue Sword that was wielded by Aerin and with inspiration from Aerin herself, a legendary hero who killed dragons and led the Damarians in battle. *The Hero and the Crown* tells the story of Aerin as she grows from an insecure adolescent into a killer of dragons. The first dragons she kills are not much bigger than dogs. Eventually, however, she kills the great dragon Maur, takes on her uncle Agsded, and saves Damar from the northern invaders.

Because of its explicit references to sex, *Deerskin* is usually classified as adult fantasy. However, it is often recommended for young adults. Deerskin, whose real name is Lissla Lissar, mentions Aerin's battle against Maur, and like Aerin, Deerskin faces a dragon and other beasts. After being raped by her own father, Deerskin travels through the mountains with her dog Ash, surviving in a hut for several years. When she almost dies, she has a vision of the Lady, a mythological figure associated with the Moon, who tells her that she will live and that she has a destiny to fulfill. Before the novel ends, Deerskin herself becomes a kind of mythological figure as she finally comes to grips with the horrors of her past.

p.102
p.45
p.204

In 1982 Robin McKinley's *The Blue Sword* was named **Newbery Honor Book** as one of the best books for children of 1981. Four years later, *The Hero and the Crown* won the **American Library Association's** **Newbery Medal**, awarded to the most distinguished work of children's literature published in the United States in the preceding year. In 1986 Bowdoin College awarded McKinley an **honorary doctorate** degree, and she received a similar honor from Wilson College in Pennsylvania ten years later.

– Richard Tuerk

Beauty and the Beast, the Movie

Jean Cocteau was a French poet, playwright, novelist, and painter, but his most accessible work is in film. He chose Madame Marie Leprince de Beaumont's 1757 fairy tale as the basis for his 1947 French film. It is considered a remarkable film, even today, because of the visual techniques Cocteau uses to tell the tale (since popularized in a Disney musical and animated film). Cocteau was a Surrealist, a follower of an artistic school that produced fantastic images by using unnatural elements. In this film, Cocteau's Surrealist touches include a statue that is alive, candelabras held by human arms projecting from walls, a chair with human arms that try to grab Beauty when she sits, and statues with human faces and eyes

that watch Beauty. Many scenes in the film look like paintings. Even to today's filmgoer, accustomed to costly special effects, Cocteau's more primitive visuals remain impressive.

Patricia MacLachlan

Born: March 3, 1938; Cheyenne, Wyoming

www.harperchildrens.com/authorintro/
index.asp?authorid=12425

Although **Patricia MacLachlan** intended her short, simply written novels for middle school students, her series that began with *Sarah, Plain and Tall* has captivated young adult readers and adults as well. One reason for the broad appeal of her books is their realism. Another is that her books do not simply focus on young narrators but explore the feelings of characters of all ages.

Patricia MacLachlan was born in Cheyenne, Wyoming, and later lived in Minnesota. An only child, she often read and discussed books with her parents, both of whom were teachers. However, she did not think she herself could ever be a writer. After graduating from the University of Connecticut in 1962, she married Robert MacLachlan, a clinical psychologist. She then began teaching at a junior high school in Manchester, Connecticut. After her three children were old enough to go off to school, she cast around for a new project. One day while she was taking a cello lesson, she suddenly realized that what she really wanted was to write for children.

MacLachlan's first publication, a picture book, appeared in 1979. Her next work was the novel *Arthur, for the Very First Time* (1980). Sev-

Mail-order Bride

The term "mail-order bride" describes women from economically depressed countries who correspond with men in wealthier countries via letter writing, or penpal services, and then later marry these men. This has also occurred frequently in the settlement of new, remote territories where men outnumber women. Today, mail-order brides commonly come from developing countries to marry men in developed countries such as the U.S.A., Canada, Australia, New Zealand, Germany, and the United Kingdom. The U.S. government has made the law allowing mail-order brides to enter the country more difficult in recent years. This is to make certain that the women who get papers to enter and stay in the U.S. actually marry and stay married to a U.S. citizen.

eral years and a number of books later, MacLachlan decided to write a love story. The result was her most complex work, *Unclaimed Treasures*. MacLachlan admits that she sees herself in the book's eleven-year-old heroine, Willa, who yearns to be unusual. Willa falls passionately in love with a next-door neighbor, an artist whose wife has left him. Eventually, however, the artist gets back together with his wife, and Willa discovers that her true love is the artist's son. The book is filled with interesting characters of all ages, including unmarried sisters who are the "unclaimed treasures" of the title.

MacLachlan's mother once told her about a member of their family who sent to Maine for a wife. That family story so impressed MacLachlan that she made one of the characters in *Arthur, for the Very First Time* a **mail-order bride**. Later a family trip to the Midwest inspired her to write another novel about a mail-order bride. She set that book in the nineteenth century, when the Midwest was filled with **homesteaders**. In *Sarah, Plain and Tall*, Sarah Houghton answers a newspaper advertisement, leaves Maine, and goes to Kansas to meet a widower who needs a wife and a mother for his three children. The book ends happily when Sarah finds love with the man and decides to stay.

p.450

Homesteader

A homesteader is someone who, upon settling on public lands, seeks to gain title to them. Homesteaders played an important role in the early history of the United States. As the population of the U.S. grew and lands west of the Mississippi River were acquired, many in government wanted to make this new land available to Americans. In 1862, the Homestead Act was passed into law. Beginning January 1, 1863, anyone intending to become a citizen who was twenty-one years of age or older could acquire a tract of land for a ten dollar registration fee. After five years of continuous residence, title went to the settler. Alternately, after six months, the settler could buy the land for $1.25 per acre. The Homestead Act was never the success it was hoped to be. Of the nearly three million homesteaders, fewer than half stayed the five years and filed claims to the land. Those who stayed were responsible for taming the American frontier.

Unclaimed Treasures was named both a 1984 Boston Globe-Horn Book Honor Book for fiction and an American Library Association **Notable Children's Book**. Among the many awards won by *Sarah, Plain and Tall* were the Scott O'Dell Award for Historical Fiction, the **Golden Kite Award**, and the prestigious **Newbery Medal**.

p.747

p.4

p.51

p.102

p.1

Patricia MacLachlan has also written scripts for three popular television movies: *Sarah, Plain and Tall* in 1991; the sequel, *Skylark*, in 1993; and, in 1999, *Winter's End*, which was later published in book form as *Caleb's Story*. In July, 2002, *Sarah, Plain and Tall* opened in a New York theater as a one-act musical. The fact that these productions all attracted broad audiences suggests that MacLachlan's novels are so true to life that they appeal to people of all ages.

– Rosemary M. Canfield Reisman

Larry McMurtry

Born: June 3, 1936; Wichita Falls, Texas

www.bookreporter.com/authors/au-mcmurtry-larry.asp

One of Texas's best-known fiction writers, **Larry McMurtry** was born into a family of cattle ranchers in north central Texas. As a young boy, he helped his father and uncles as a **cowhand** and grew up listening to family stories of cowboys and the West. The Texas landscape colors much of his fiction, but as a child, he was more interested in reading than ranching. He majored in English in college and earned a master's degree from Rice University in Texas, where he took creative writing classes. After he graduated, he was awarded a **Wallace Stegner Fellowship**, which allowed him to pursue writing at Stanford University in California with Stegner, one of the masters of Western literature.

Horseman, Pass By, Leaving Cheyenne, and *The Last Picture Show,* McMurtry's first three novels, are often referred to as the Thalia trilogy after the fictitious Texas town in which they are set, which McMurtry based on his hometown of Archer City. The most popular of these novels, *The Last Picture Show,* is an attempt to dispel the myths of the romance of small western towns. It depicts the residents of Thalia as mean and stupid and life there as threadbare and worn out. The novel is concerned with the coming of age of adolescents who are struggling to mature in the suffocating and confining atmosphere of a small town.

McMurtry's next three books move out of the countryside and into the city; for this reason they are often called the urban trilogy. *Moving On, All My Friends Are Going to Be Strangers,* and *Terms of En-*

452

453

TITLES

Horseman, Pass By, 1961

Leaving Cheyenne, 1963

The Last Picture Show, 1966

Moving On, 1970

All My Friends Are Going to Be Strangers, 1972

Terms of Endearment, 1975

Somebody's Darling, 1978

Cadillac Jack, 1982

The Desert Rose, 1983

Lonesome Dove, 1985

Texasville, 1987

Anything for Billy, 1988

Some Can Whistle, 1989

Buffalo Girls, 1990

The Evening Star, 1992

Streets of Laredo, 1993

Pretty Boy Floyd, 1994 (with Diana Ossana)

Dead Man's Walk, 1995

The Late Child, 1995

Comanche Moon, 1997

Cowhand

A cowhand or cowboy is someone who tends to a herd of cattle. This tradition came to North America with the Spanish settlers. It continued in the Old West where open rangeland was used to graze cattle. As land came under private ownership, cowhands fenced the land to keep cattle from roaming into other private lands. They branded cattle with the ranch's brand, a symbol registered and unique to a particular owner. Today, the number of working cowhands in the U.S. has decreased substantially, but the image of the tough cowboy lives on.

dearment are set in Houston. *Terms of Endearment* became the most popular of the three. This novel concerns Aurora Greenway and her difficult relationship with her married daughter, Emma.

McMurtry also wrote another three books that form a trio of historical Westerns. In these novels he shows the characters of the Old West for what he believed they really were—the sad inhabitants of a dying era. *Lonesome Dove*, which became a bestseller soon after it was released, follows the adventures of three former Texas Rangers as they drive a herd of cattle from Lonesome Dove in Texas north to the Montana Territory. *Anything for Billy* is a retelling of the legend of the outlaw Billy the Kid. *Buffalo Girls* also deals with historical characters, including Calamity Jane, Wild Bill Hickok, Buffalo Bill Cody, and Sitting Bull as they travel together in Buffalo Bill's Wild West Show toward the end of their careers.

Many of Larry McMurtry's novels have been made into popular films for the big screen and television. The most notable of these screen adaptations include *Hud* (which was adapted from McMurtry's first novel, *Horseman, Pass By*); *Terms of Endear-*

p.11
p.38

ment; *Lonesome Dove*; and *The Last Picture Show*—all of which won honors and became classics in their own right. Among the many writing awards won by McMurtry are the **Pulitzer Prize** for fiction for *Lonesome Dove* and an **Academy Award** for his screenplay of *The Last Picture Show*.

– Deborah DePiero

p.137

Wallace Stegner Fellowship

The Stanford Creative Writing Program at Stanford University in Palo Alto, California, offers ten fellowships each year for the two-year writing program, five in fiction and five in poetry. At any given time, there are twenty fellows enrolled in the program. Named for writer Wallace Stegner, the fellowship offers $22,000 per year in living expenses plus full tuition. The program offers no degree and does not require fellows to attend classes. The emerging writers are selected for their artistic promise, do not have to have a degree, and are considered to be working artists while at the campus. They attend workshops with other fellows and faculty twice a week and work on their creative writing the rest of the time.

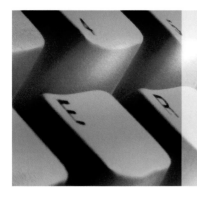

Margaret Mahy

Born: March 21, 1936; Whakatane, New Zealand

library.christchurch.org.nz/childrens/
margaretmahy/about.asp

Margaret Mahy was a librarian for many years before she became a prolific writer for children and young adults. Her books for younger readers are wide-ranging and highly imaginative, and her young adult fiction, though much more tightly focused, displays the same inventiveness. Her early work for young adults uses supernatural and science-fiction themes to dramatize the difficulties faced by adolescents in unusual and sometimes dysfunctional families. Even in such naturalistic thrillers as *Memory* and *Underrunners* she sustains a feverish narrative intensity that edges into hallucination.

The Haunting is an unorthodox account of the impact on a supernaturally talented child of the discovery that he is the victim of a hereditary "curse." The curse's management requires the boy to reconcile the conflicting factions of his family. The similarly gifted heroine of *The Changeover* must fight to save her brother from a psychic vampire. Both these novels won Great Britain's **Carnegie Medal**, and their themes are carried forward in three further novels. Of these, *The Tricksters* is the most ambitious and the most intricate. *Dangerous Spaces*, a similar story, features a heroine seduced by a ghost. *Alchemy* is a tightly focused thriller, whose hero must attain rapid mastery of his extraordinary powers of perception if he is to defy the predator who wants to use him to exploit a similarly gifted girl. *Alchemy* is strengthened by the science-fiction logic behind its supernatural phenomena.

p.3

p.455

p.30

p.4

Heredity

Heredity is the process in which genetic characteristics are passed down from generation to generation. The characteristics may be either physical or biological. Physical chacteristics include hair color, eye color, and skin color. Biological characteristics include a higher chance of developing many diseases such  as Alzheimer's, breast cancer, color blindness, and sickle-cell disease. Advances in genetic mapping, such as the Human Genome Project, provide knowledge about the genetics underlying different inherited diseases. This should increase opportunities for diagnosis, prevention, and treatment of inherited diseases.

Memory and *Alchemy* both have romantic subplots that Mahy handles with considerable delicacy and conviction. Her novels in which the difficulties of teenage sexual relationships are placed in the foreground are exceptionally well done. For example, *The Catalogue of the Universe* and *Twenty-four Hours* both describe attempts to form personal relationships under difficult circumstances.

Most of Mahy's young protagonists come from homes that are broken in one way or another. Many live in houses that are in dire need of repair, situated at the ends of dirt roads, adjacent to dangerous headlands projecting out into the sea. Although such settings have a realistic basis in the local geography of Mahy's New Zealand home, they also fulfill a powerful symbolic function in her work. In *Underrunners* the setting combines with the spontaneously generated subterranean traps that give the novel its title. Family life, in the world of Mahy's fiction, never conforms to the model of the comfortable nuclear family. Secrets that parents withhold from their children—often unwittingly, or with the best of motives—are ticking time bombs whose defusing usually requires

New Zealand

New Zealand is located in the southwest Pacific Ocean, midway between the equator and the icy Antarctic. Its closest continental neighbor, Australia, lies more than 1,000 miles to the northwest. New Zealand consists of two main islands, North Island and South Island, which are separated by the Cook Strait. A third, much smaller island, Stewart Island, sits to the south of South Island. New Zealand has gained international recognition for its antinuclear policy. With widespread support from the public, the fourth Labour government declared New Zealand a nuclear-free zone in 1984. Its antinuclear policy, along with its natural beauty, low population, and rural-based economy, has earned New Zealand a reputation as a "clean and green" country.

heroic measures. However, her leading characters always meet their challenges in a thoroughly plausible and graceful fashion, which is the measure of Mahy's power as a story-teller.

– Brian Stableford

Jan Mark

Born: June 22, 1943; Welwyn, Hertfordshire, England

www.geocities.com/beatrix.olaerts/janmark/jan.html

Jan Mark was born Janet Marjorie Brisland in southeastern England, where she was educated at a grammar school in Kent and at Canterbury College of Art. She spent the early years of her married life in a Norfolk village before eventually settling in Oxford. All these settings are recalled in her work, which has an unusually acute sense of place.

Thunder and Lightnings, Mark's **Carnegie Medal**-winning first novel, is a tale of friendship mediated by obsession—a theme that recurs frequently in her other stories featuring adolescents absorbed in quirky projects and interests. The spectrum of such interests featured in her work is unusually wide, including amateur archaeology in *Under the Autumn Garden*, motorbikes in *Handles* and American football in *Man in Motion*.

p.42

Mark's most ambitious early works are the science-fiction novels *The Ennead, Divide and Rule* and the **fantasy** *Aquarius*, all of which feature harsh settings and manipulatively authoritarian societies. Much of her later work has dealt with domestic and school life, but she never abandoned her ambition to deal with large themes. She returned to that kind of fiction in *The Hillingdon Fox*, which cleverly juxtaposes diaries recording the **Falkland Islands** and Gulf Wars.

p.87

458

Much of Mark's best work, from the stories collected in *Nothing to Be Afraid Of* in 1980 to her later work, has been in short forms. She skillfully constructs delicate slice-of-life stories, exceptional examples of which can be found in *Enough Is Too*

TITLES

Thunder and Lightnings, 1976

Under the Autumn Garden, 1977

The Ennead, 1978

Divide and Rule, 1979

Nothing to Be Afraid Of, 1980

Hairs in the Palm of the Hand, 1981

The Long Distance Poet, 1981

Aquarius, 1982

The Dead Letter Box, 1982

Feet and Other Stories, 1983

Handles, 1983

At the Sign of the Dog and Rocket, 1985

Trouble Half-Way, 1985

Frankie's Hat, 1986

Dream House, 1987

Enough Is Too Much Already, 1988

Man in Motion, 1989

A Can of Worms and Other Stories, 1990

Finders, Losers, 1990

In Black and White, 1991

The Hillingdon Fox, 1991

Much Already and *Frankie's Hat.* Her collections sometimes have a unity, as in *Finders, Losers*, whose six stories share the same setting and whose narrative puzzles interlock, or *They Do Things Differently There*, which consists of character studies of the charming inhabitants of the eccentric village of Compton Rosehay. *A Can of Worms and Other Stories* focuses on more bizarre aspects of teenage life, while *In Black and White* consists of tales of the supernatural.

Although a few of Mark's longer works seem rather slight, as if they grew from short stories by sheer force of detail–*The Lady with Iron Bones* is one such—her best novels are artfully layered. *A Fine Summer Knight* and *The Sighting* are mysteries involving glimpses of things that are not what they appear to be. *Heathrow Nights* is a complex story whose **protagonist**, excluded from a school trip, hides out at **Heathrow Airport**, where lack of sleep delivers him into a hallucinatory recapitulation of his father's death and his mother's remarriage, fil-

p.23

p.459

Falkland Islands War

The dispute between Britain and Argentina over possession of the Falkland Islands had persisted since 1831, when the U.S. intervened to allow the British to reoccupy the islands. In December, 1981, tired of negotiation and struggling with internal problems, the Argentine government (which was headed by a group of military officers) decided to invade the Falklands. President Leopoldo Galtieri assumed that the United States would support his decision, while Foreign Minister Niconar Costa Méndez assumed that the British would not retaliate. They were both wrong.

The Falklands War was a "little war"–the British did not use their nuclear weapons or attack the Argentine mainland. Some scoffed at the conflict, calling it "two bald men fighting over a comb," while others insisted that the invasion of April 2, 1982, was an unjustified blow that forced the British to become involved. An immediate effect in Argentina was that Galtieri lost his place as president; the British people, meanwhile, were delighted by their victory, which may have helped Margaret Thatcher get reelected in 1983.

tered through the imagery of William Shakespeare's play *Hamlet* (pr. 1600-1601).

The Eclipse of the Century is a novel whose young hero is drawn by a near-death experience to the Central Asian town of Qantoum. There he finds that the pagan tribesmen of the Sturyat have been waiting for five hundred years—most recently amid the rubble of the shattered Soviet Union—for a messiah. His arrival starts a crisis that inexorably turns to disaster as more **apocalyptic** cultists arrive in search of the impossible.

Jan Mark's ability to weave intellectually challenging material into the texture of everyday adolescent life is the essence of her artistry. In addition to the **Carnegie Medal** she won for *Thunder and Lightnings* in 1976, she won the same award for *Handles* in 1983.

— Brian Stableford

John Marsden

Born: September 27, 1950; Melbourne, Victoria, Australia

www.panmacmillan.com.au/johnmarsden/index.htm

John Marsden's award-winning novels are about children and adolescents who face difficult situations that typically involve domestic violence and dysfunctional families. His troubled characters often tell their stories in diary form, providing authentic voices for their perspectives on difficult subjects.

Marsden was born in Melbourne, **Australia**, p.46 and spent most of his youth in Sydney, where he attended a prestigious private school with a military atmosphere. A passionate reader, he wrote short books and circulated his underground newspaper about new rock bands while he was still in school. Around the time he was fifteen, he noticed that there seemed to be little literature written for adolescents. When he read J. D. Salinger's novel *The Catcher in the Rye* (1951), he was captivated by what he regarded as a genuine contemporary teenage voice. He later insisted that his own success in capturing youthful voices in his book came from reading Salinger's novel.

After dropping out of the University of Sydney, Marsden submitted a novel to a publisher; it was rejected. Following a series of odd jobs, he slipped into such a deep depression that he ended up in a psychiatric institution. There he met a fourteen-year-old girl who would not speak to anyone, but on her last day at the institution, he managed to talk with her. Her plight became the inspiration for *So Much to Tell*

You, a novel about a girl who is **mute** until a teacher breaks into her silent world. Written in diary format, the story relates the girl's physical abuse.

Marsden caused controversy with *Letters from the Inside*, a novel about two girls who are pen pals. One is in prison and the other implies her brother may have attacked her. In *Dear Miffy*, an institutionalized teenage boy named Tony writes a series of letters to his girlfriend, Miffy. However, he never mails the letters, which recount the couple's turbulent relationship against a background of sex, violence, and dysfunctional families.

Marsden's long-time fantasy of a world without adults was developed into a series of adventure stories about an invasion of Australia. In *Tomorrow, When the War Began*, a group of teenagers return from a camping trip in the bush to discover that everyone in their town has been captured by a foreign military force, leaving them on their own. The group organizes to fight the invaders, leading to additional books, *The Dead of Night* and *The Third Day, the Frost*, that detail the teenagers fighting the invaders. In 1996,

Australia

Located between the Indian and Pacific Oceans, Australia is earth's smallest continent. It is an island and the only continent occupied by a single nation, the Commonwealth of Australia. It is also the flattest and driest continent, with two-thirds of its mass either desert or semiarid. Because of its geographical isolation from other world land masses, Australia is home to a number of unique plant, animal, and bird species. When British explorer Captain Cook landed in Australia in 1788, he discovered an island inhabited by some 300,000 Aborigines belonging to some 650 tribes. Britain later began colonizing the land with convicts freed from its overcrowded prisons. Today, some nineteen million people of varied cultures and ethnicities populate the country.

Marsden wrote a fourth novel, *Darkness, Be My Friend*, and a fifth, *Burning for Revenge* (1997) in this series.

Marsden continues to provide voices for the voiceless victims in *Checkers*, a novel about an unnamed girl talking to her dog as she recuperates from a breakdown in a mental hospital. The first-person flashbacks relate the girl's father's participation in criminal activities while she tries to understand, as any teenager would, her parent's behavior and motives.

One of Australia's most popular and **best-selling** authors, John Marsden has been awarded numerous awards in Australia. The American Library Association named *Tomorrow, When the War Began* one of its **Best Books for Young Adults**, and *So Much to Tell You* won a **Christopher Award**.

– Mary Hurd

p.38
p.4
p.480

Speech Disorders

Speech disorders fall into various categories: problems speaking (such as stuttering), difficulty articulating sounds, and the lack of ability to use language. These disorders have been known since antiquity and although they are frequently hereditary, the genetic cause is often unclear. Often times there are psychological reasons for them. The cures for all types of speech disorders vary. They require the participation of teachers in school systems and the attention of professionals such as speech therapists, audiologists, surgeons, and psychiatrists. Each case must be analyzed carefully and then treated individually. The success of the treatment varies from patient to patient, regardless of the disorder, the therapeutic procedures used, or the therapists involved.

Victor Martinez

Born: 1954; Fresno, California

www.harpercollins.com/global_scripts/product_catalog/author_xml.asp?/authorid=12450

464

p.233

The characters who populate **Victor Martinez**'s award-winning novel are realistically drawn Mexican Americans who struggle to survive in a housing project in the central valley of California. While the challenges Manuel, the fourteen-year-old protagonist, faces in this novel are influenced by race and culture, the crises and experiences he faces: violence, love, sibling rivalry and loyalty, jealousy, the need to belong, and discrimination—all topics to which teenagers can relate.

Victor Martinez was born and raised in central California, the fourth son of twelve children. His parents, who met in a migrant labor camp, raised their family in a housing project, a setting that forms the background in *Parrot in the Oven*. In a form similar to a series of vignettes, Martinez explores a young Mexican American boy's poignant coming of age in a world fraught with poverty, abuse, limited job opportunities, and unequal educational opportunities. Martinez employs the immediacy and authenticity of the first-person point of view to explore Manuel's life experiences as he struggles to find himself and establish an identity within his dysfunctional family and within a community that is marginalized and disenfranchised.

The problems that confront Manuel's family in a housing project sometimes seem overwhelming. His father is an abusive alcoholic, who would rather

p.632

p.101

TITLE

Parrot in the Oven: Mi Vida, 1996

Housing project

A housing project, more commonly called public housing, is usually a block of low-income housing that is operated by a government agency. In the 1930's, the trend to develop public housing began and it continues to the present. However, many of the original houses or buildings have been destroyed or renovated due to poor upkeep and inadequate management of the buildings, leading to high crime rates. Today, public housing continues to have a reputation for high crime, drug use, and prostitution.

have his family starve than accept welfare. Eventually he is jailed for threatening Manuel's mother with a rifle. His older brother Nardo is as irresponsible as his father. Nardo cannot hold a job and seems to be following in his father's footsteps by drinking every night. His oldest sister Magda performs back-breaking labor in a laundry. Her attempts to cope with her environment result in pregnancy and a tragic miscarriage. Manuel's mother is the force that keeps the family together. However, she has an obsession with cleaning her home, as if by cleaning she can eradicate the family problems.

Unsure of the role he plays in his own family, Manuel looks for acceptance outside his home. Even there, however, he encounters problems. His neighbors, the Garcia brothers, make fun of him. Some of his Anglo schoolmates insult him because he is poor and throw ethnic slurs at him. Even one of his teachers regards him as a charity case. An event that tests his courage and his sense of self is his initiation into a gang, the traditional model of masculinity ascribed to young Mexican American men. Although Manuel needs a group with which to identify, he rejects the group when they steal an innocent woman's purse. His compassion for the woman and his sense of justice will not allow him to participate in the robbery.

Victor Martinez has written a gripping, compassionate story about one boy's journey to discover his place in his world. His poetic, often visual language not only reinforces Manuel's frustrations and bitterness as he copes with his environment but also the love Martinez has for the people who inhabit his world. *Parrot in the Oven* earned several awards, including the **National Book Award** for Young People's Literature, the **Pura Belpré Medal**, and the **Americas Award for Children's and Young Adult Literature**.

p.122

p.465

– Sharon K. Wilson

Pura Belpré Medal

The Pura Belpré Medal was established in 1996 in honor of Pura Belpré, the first Latina librarian from New York Public Library. Pura Belpré is recognized for her work in preserving Puerto Rican folklore as a storyteller, librarian, and author. Two awards are presented every other year, one to a Latino/Latina author and one to a Latino/Latina illustrator whose work makes an outstanding contribution to children's literature by portraying, affirming, and celebrating Latino cultural experience.

Toshi Maruki

Born: February 11, 1912; Hokkaido, Japan
Died: January 13, 2000; Saitama, Japan

www.harperchildrens.com/global_scripts/product_
catalog/author_xml.asp?authorID=17599

TITLE

Hiroshima No Pika, 1980

Toshi Maruki was an artist and children's book **illustrator** whose picture book on the dropping of the first atomic bomb on the city of Hiroshima, Japan, during World War II resembles a children's book but is actually most appropriate for young adults. Libraries often shelve *Hiroshima No Pika* in their children's sections, but Maruki's watercolor paintings and story are not for young children. Her book features graphic images of war, death, and suffering, and is recommended for those over age twelve. Maruki wrote the book in the hope that atomic weapons would never again be used on anyone, anywhere. Her book presents a powerful message for nuclear disarmament and world peace. Why write a children's book about such a horrifying event? Maruki wanted to tell young people about something bad that happened in the hope that their knowing will keep it from happening again.

When the United States dropped an atomic bomb on **Hiroshima** on August 6, 1945, thirty-three-year-old Toshi Maruki and her husband, Iri, were in Tokyo. When they heard the news of the bomb, they immediately went to Hiroshima, where their family lived, to help however they

p.3

p.467

John Hersey's *Hiroshima*

John Hersey's *Hiroshima* was first published as a magazine article in *The New Yorker* magazine in 1946, just a year after the end of World War II. It was a non-fiction account of six survivors of the atomic blast in Hiroshima and their life afterwards. The article aroused a lot of attention for its realistic report of the devastation and was soon published in book form by Alfred A. Knopf. Within the next year *Hiroshima* was translated into more than thirty languages and was in circulation around the world.

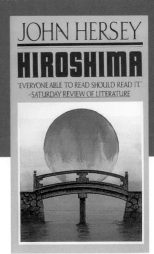

could. There they found Toshi's uncle and two nieces dead and a younger sister suffering from severe burns. Maruki's father died six months later of radiation sickness. The Marukis helped move the injured, cremate the dead, and scavenge for food. With death all around them, they wandered through the ruins in horror and disbelief.

Maruki and her husband dedicated the rest of their lives to making the reality of the devastation of the atomic bomb known and remembered. They began to paint what they had seen in Hiroshima, creating together the Hiroshima Murals. While Maruki was at an exhibition of pictures depicting the atomic bomb, a woman came out of the crowd and told her personal story: how she had tried to escape the flash of Hiroshima carrying her wounded husband on her back and leading her child by the hand. Her story became the basis of *Hiroshima No Pika*.

The book opens with seven-year-old Mii having breakfast in her Hiroshima home with her mother and father. Suddenly a terrible orange-white flash, followed by shock waves and fire, strikes the city. The atomic bomb has been dropped. Mii is knocked unconscious. Her mother pulls her badly hurt husband out of the flames, lifts him onto her back, takes Mii's hand, and begins to run. They join crowds of people heading for the river, fleeing the Flash, their

Mildred L. Batchelder Award

The Mildred L. Batchelder Award was established in 1966 in honor of Mildred L. Batchelder, a former executive director of the Association for Library Service to Children (ALSC), a division of the American Library Association. She made a lasting contribution to literature by encouraging the translation of children's books from other countries. This award is therefore given to an American publisher for an outstanding contribution in international exchange through the translation and publication of a book previously published in a foreign language in a foreign country. The ALSC gives out this award to encourage more publishers to seek out children's books that have made a contribution in other parts of the world and to encourage communication between cultures.

clothing burned away. Dead and dying people lie everywhere. A swallow hops by them; its wings are burned and it cannot fly. In a single moment, Hiroshima has become a burned-out wasteland. Mii's life becomes a nightmare, and her father later dies of radiation sickness.

Among the many awards that Toshi Maruki's book won are the **Mildred L. Batchelder Award** and a **Boston Globe-Horn Honor Book** award. *Hiroshima No Pika* also won the **Ehon Nippon Prize** for the best picture book in Japan. The book's illustrations are even more important than its text. Painting the horror of nuclear war was Maruki's mission. Her full-color images are graphic, thought-provoking, and powerful.

– Susan Butterworth

 p.747

 p.46

Sharon Bell Mathis

Born: February 16, 1937; Atlantic City, New Jersey

TITLES

Listen for the Fig Tree, 1974

The Hundred Penny Box, 1975

Running Girl: The Diary of Ebonee Rose, 1997

Sharon Bell Mathis has filled a gap in literature that she felt during her own childhood by creating books with sympathetic, recognizable African American characters for children and young adults. She is particularly adept at combining history with contemporary stories to offer situations with which her readers can identify, while introducing them to African American history.

Mathis was born in New Jersey and grew up in the Bedford-Stuyvesant area of Brooklyn, New York. Her mother was a poet and **illustrator** who loved books and filled their home with them. She also encouraged her children to read and visit the library often, and Mathis remembers being disappointed at not finding African American children like herself in the books she found in the library. After studying **library science** at the Catholic University of America, she became a **librarian** at the Patricia Roberts Harris Educational Center.

One of Mathis's most successful books is her inspirational biography of the **jazz** great, **Ray Charles**. In it she chronicles the challenges faced by Charles, who became totally blind at the age of six and was sent away from his family to a school for the blind. By the time he graduated at fifteen, both of his parents and his brother had died. Despite these seemingly insurmountable setbacks, Charles went on to a legendary career in music.

In Mathis's fictional *The Hundred Penny Box*, Michael's great-great-aunt Dewbet Thomas comes to live with his family. She has a special box contain-

p.38

p.134

p.405

p.35

p.470

ing one penny for each of her one hundred years, and Michael loves to hear the stories she tells as she pulls out each penny and recalls that year in her life. However, Michael's mother grows impatient with Aunt Dew and throws out many of her possessions. Michael then makes it his responsibility to protect the hundred-penny box and the stories of the past it holds.

Running Girl: The Diary of Ebonee Rose covers twenty days in the life of eleven-year-old runner Ebonee Rose as she prepares for a city track meet. Her diary chronicles the days leading up to the meet, describing her training regimen, her fears, and her

Ray Charles

Ray Charles, who died in 2004 at the age of seventy-three, is considered one of the most successful and influential musicians in U.S. history. Charles is credited with popularizing the blues tradition. With his unique voice and sophisticated piano playing, he also helped create soul music by merging blues with gospel, and he expanded the scope of country and western music. Charles grew up in exteme poverty in northern Florida. When he was only five, he saw his younger brother drown. Shortly thereafter, Charles began to lose his eyesight. By age seven he was completely blind, and he was enrolled in St. Augustine's School for the Deaf and Blind in Orlando. His father died when he was ten, his mother when he was fifteen. Shortly thereafter, he left school to pursue a life of music. Truly an American institution, Charles has left his fans a legacy of wonderful songs from all genres of popular music.

Wilma Rudolph

It is not uncommon for an athlete to overcome illness or injury, but for Wilma Glodean Rudolph, the obstacles were staggering. Born in 1940, she became ill at age four with pneumonia and scarlet fever, which caused her left leg to become weakened and deformed. Denied access to the best doctors and hospitals because she was African American, Wilma was cared for by her mother and siblings, who all helped by massaging her legs and driving her to therapy. By age eleven she was out of a leg brace and playing basketball at school. She became an excellent athlete. While attending high school, Wilma was encouraged to take up track. With her relay teammates, sixteen-year-old Wilma attended the 1956 Olympics in Melbourne, Australia, and won a bronze medal. Four years later in Rome, she won gold in the 100-meter dash, the 200-meter dash, and the 4 x 100-meter relay. Wilma became the first American woman to win three gold medals in an Olympics.

relationships with her teammates. She also writes about her heroes, notable African American women runners and track stars of the past, such as Wilma Rudolph, Jackie Joyner-Kersee, and Gail Devers. The book, which includes a photograph of each of her heroes, combines history with an appealing contemporary story.

Sharon Bell Mathis received the **Coretta Scott King Award** for *Ray Charles* and *The Hundred Penny Box* received **Boston-Horn Globe Honor Book** and **Newbery Honor Book** awards. *Listen for the Fig Tree* was an **American Library Association Notable Book**. Mathis is a founding member of the children's literature division of the Washington, D.C., Black Writer's Workshop.

— Mary Virginia Davis

471

p.66

747

p.45

p.102

William Mayne

Born: March 16, 1928; Kingston upon Hull, England

www.davidhigham.co.uk/html/clients/Mayne

William Mayne is an English writer whose remarkable career has spanned more than fifty years and one hundred books (the majority of them for younger readers), without the slightest loss of imagination or intelligence. Although he has used such devices as treasure hunts and timeslips many times over, he has never repeated himself and has always continued to break new ground, as in the romantic subplot of *Midnight Fair* and a colorful expansion of the famous folktale of the Lambton Worm, *The Worm in the Well*.

Mayne has lived in northern England's Yorkshire Dales for most of his life and has set many of his novels there, but he was educated at the Cathedral Choir School in southern England's **Canterbury**. p.473 That experience provided the background for four of his early novels: *A Swarm in May, Choristers' Cake, Cathedral Wednesday* and *Words and Music*, and continued to echo in later works such as the fine dark fantasies *It* and *Cuddy*. His early plots, from *Follow the Footprints* through *The World Upside Down, Underground Alley, The Rolling Season* and *The Thumbstick* to *The Twelve Dancers*, were usually configured as treasure hunts, although the eventual discoveries are usually more important as lessons than riches, as in the sentimental **Carnegie** p.4[?] **Medal**-winning *A Grass Rope*.

The exploits of the characters in *Sand* and *Pig*

in the Middle come to life through the quirky dialogue that became Mayne's hallmark, but the device worked even better when he began to provide more challenging topics of conversation, as in the mysteries *The Battlefield*, *Ravensgill*, *Royal Harry* and *The Incline*, and even more so in the fine timeslip fantasies *Earthfasts* and *Over the Hills and Far Away*, all of which brought the problems of adolescence into focus. Mayne's finest works of this kind are *A Game of Dark*, whose hero must find a solution to his problems in visions, and *The Jersey Shore*, which places an adolescent's life in 1930's America side by side with an old man's regretful reminiscences of his family history in England.

These books brought to maturity a fascination with bleak landscapes that is reflected in much of Mayne's later work, often fantasized, as in the fine novellas "Boy to Island" and "Stony Ray" (both in *All the King's Men*) and two belated sequels to *Earthfasts*, *Cradlefasts* and *Candlefasts*. Mayne is prepared to go far and wide in search of such landscapes. *Salt River Times* is set in **Australia**, *Drift* in p.461 the ancient North American wilderness and *Tiger's Railway* in Eastern Europe. *Winter Quarters* describes the odyssey of a company of fairground folk in search of a haven, while the **Carnegie Medal**-winning *Low Tide* is a stirring historical adventure

Canterbury Cathedral

Canterbury Cathedral was founded in Britain in 597 B.C.E. with the arrival of St. Augustine, the first archbishop from Rome. However, the earlist part of the present structure is the great Romanesque crypt built circa 1100. The Gothic choir built on top of the crypt was constructed after the original was destroyed by fire in 1174. The Cathedral has withstood a series of events including the sack of Henry VIII and the bombs of World War II. The Cathedral is also site of the murder of Thomas Becket, whose tomb still lies in Trinity Chapel.

p.456

p.47

story set in **New Zealand** in the aftermath of a **tsunami** tidal wave. A sentimental story of a brain-damaged boy who finds employment opening lock gates on a canal, *Gideon Ahoy!* and an offbeat **fantasy** whose infant hero is kidnapped by eagles and taught to fly, *Antar and the Eagles*, also make use of environmental detail.

p.87

– Brian Stableford

Tsunami

A tsunami occurs when a shock is administered to coastal waters, usually from an underwater earthquake. A tsunami is often the chief reason for deaths as heavily populated coastal areas are swamped with sudden, gigantic waves. Without early warning, towns and villages, and whole buildings and their entire contents can be swept away by the power of such waves. Most of the large tsunami that have resulted in major loss of life have occurred in the Pacific basin and have been the result of earthquakes caused by shifting tectonic plates along the western shore of the Pacific Ocean. Japan has frequently been the scene of tsunami, but they have also occurred in Indonesia, eastern Russia, and Alaska. On Sunday, December 26, 2004, a 9.0 magnitude earthquake struck around 7:00 A.M. deep beneath the Indian Ocean, about 100 miles from the western coast of Indonesia's Sumatra island. The resulting tsunami wiped out coastal areas in Indonesia, Sri Lanka, Thailand, India, Somalia, and the eastern shores of Africa. There were more than 150,000 confirmed deaths. A worldwide relief effort provided medical and emergency services and billions of dollars in financial aid, and larger nations such as Australia and the United States offered to assist in the placement of early-warning systems in the area.

Harry Mazer

Born: May 31, 1925; New York, New York

http://www.randomhouse.com/teachers/catalog/display_bio.pperl?isbn=0440947979

The adolescent characters in **Harry Mazer**'s books face moral dilemmas in realistic settings and fast-paced plots, often finding that they must rely on one another to survive. Critics praise Mazer's ability to write believably about teenage emotions, including romance, in a straightforward, readable style that has become popular with young readers.

Born in New York City in 1925, Mazer received a **Purple Heart Medal** for his service in the U.S. Army Air Force during World War II. Afterward he earned a bachelor's degree from Union College and a master's degree from Syracuse University. In 1950 he married novelist Norma Fox, who afterward published as Norma Fox Mazer. The Mazers began their writing careers producing **pulp** fiction to support their young family of four children and would go on to coauthor several juvenile novels together. Their oldest daughter, Anne, would also become a young adult novelist. Before he became a full-time writer in 1963, Harry Mazer worked as a brakeman and switchman for a railroad. He was also a construction worker, a sheet-metal worker, a welder, and an English teacher. During the 1970's, he began publishing a long list of successful adolescent novels.

The Last Mission, probably Mazer's best known and most renowned novel, stands out from his other work for its convincing portrait of fifteen-year-old

.476

p.92

TITLES

Snow Bound, 1973

The Last Mission, 1979

I Love You, Stupid!, 1981

The Island Keeper, 1981

When the Phone Rang, 1985

The Girl of His Dreams, 1987

Someone's Mother Is Missing, 1990

A Boy at War, 2001

Purple Heart Medal

During the early period of World War II, the Purple Heart medal was awarded both for wounds received in action against the enemy and for exemplary performance of duty. With the establishment of the Legion of Merit by an Act of Congress, the practice of awarding the Purple Heart for exemplary service was discontinued. However, on December 3, 1942, by Executive Order 9277, the award was extended to all United States armed services and required that regulations follow a standard of application. Today, the Purple Heart is awarded to any person wounded in action while serving in the armed forces of the United States, or to the next of kin of personnel who have been killed or died as a result of injuries received in action after April 5, 1917.

Jack Raab, a Jewish boy who borrows his older brother's identification to enlist in the army to fight against Adolf Hitler. Jack becomes a gunner in a B-17, flying night missions across Germany in 1944. p.477 Although Mazer draws on technical details of his own experience in World War II, he draws even more deeply on the emotional life of a high school freshman who is not prepared for the terrifying life of a war hero. Mazer revisited his World War II experience with *A Boy at War*. Its protagonist, fourteen-year-old Adam Pelko, has recently moved to Honolulu with his navy lieutenant father and is out at sea, fishing with classmates, when the Japanese at- p.612 tack **Pearl Harbor**. Mistaken for an enlisted man, Adam is ordered to take part in the attempts to rescue survivors even as he worries about the fate of his father.

p.23

Conflicts other than war provide opportunities for rites of passage in most Mazer novels. In *Snow Bound*, for example, Tony Laporte is angry with his parents and takes his mother's car, picks up a hitch-hiker, and crashes the car in the middle of the snowy wilderness. In *The Island Keeper*, Cleo escapes to an uninhabited island to get away from her overprotective family. *When the Phone Rang* depicts three siblings staying together after their parents are killed in an airplane crash. Similarly, in *Someone's Mother Is Missing*, Lisa Allen and her sister must cope with loss after the death of their father and abandonment by their mother. Championship runner Willis Pierce attempts to find his ideal woman in *The Girl of His Dreams*.

A number of Harry Mazer's books have been named **Best Books for Young Adults** by the **American Library Association**, and *The Last Mission* was named to the **Best of the Best Books** list for 1970-1983. *Snow Bound* was filmed as an NBC Afterschool Special.

p.480

p.45

– Lisa Rowe Fraustino

B-17

Although it first originated as a maritime bomber, the B-17, has become one of the most well-known bombers of all time. The B-17 became famous for its ability to bring home its crew despite heavy damage. The B-17 also became famous for its role during Word War II in the strategic daylight bombing raids over Germany between 1942 and 1945. With up to thirteen machine guns, the B-17 was nicknamed the "Flying Fortress." A total of 12,731 "Flying Fortresses" were produced during World War II, representing the power of American aviation.

Norma Fox Mazer

Born: May 15, 1931; New York, New York

http://www.teenreads.com/authors/au-mazer-norma.asp

Norma Fox Mazer is a prolific author of young adult novels and short stories who is known for her ability to engage adolescent themes with poignancy and literary skill. Her plots are usually realistic and depict members of families in conflict.

Born Norma Fox in New York City in 1931, Mazer taught herself to read by the time she was five. She continued to read voraciously and by the time she was thirteen, she knew she wanted to be a writer. She attended Antioch College and Syracuse University and married Harry Mazer in 1950. Afterward, both she and her husband embarked on writing careers, producing mainly **pulp-magazine fiction** to support their four children. Their oldest daughter, Anne, would also eventually become a writer.

p.479

Mazer and her husband wrote several juvenile novels together. Through their years of writing **pulp fiction**, Mazer always wanted to write novels. She claims that those early years of hard work to make a living taught her the skills a novelist needs, especially how to revise manuscripts until they tell the story the writer envisions. She wrote her first young adult novel at the urging of her agent. When it sold, she felt encouraged to write more.

p.92

Many of Mazer's books deal with rocky family relationships, from sibling rivalry, soap-opera style,

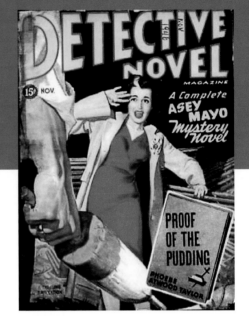

in *Three Sisters* to a quest to find the father who abandoned the fourteen-year-old heroine of *Missing Pieces*. In *Babyface* Toni Chessmore is sent to stay with her older sister after their father suffers a heart attack; her life changes when she learns shocking family secrets from which she has been sheltered all her life.

Silver and *Girlhearts*, Mazer's two books about Sarabeth Silver, trace the story of a teenager who lives in a trailer and must find friends in a new school, only to be faced with her thirty-year-old mother's sudden fatal heart attack. Sarabeth finds her way back to the relatives who disowned her mother when she became pregnant as a teenager. Abusive relationships, a theme introduced in *Silver*, are explored more fully in *When She Was Good*, the story of seventeen-year-old Em Thurkill's suffering under the control of her mentally ill older sister and her liberation after her sister's death. Critics rate *When She Was Good* and *After the Rain* among Mazer's best books.

Norma Fox Mazer has received numerous awards for her work. Many of her titles have been named **Best Books for Young Adults** by the **American Library Association**, which also

p.480

p.45

named *After the Rain* a **Newbery Honor Book** and a **Notable Book**. *Taking Terri Mueller* won the Mystery Writers of America's **Edgar Allan Poe Award** even though Mazer did not intend to write a mystery. In *Taking Terri Mueller*, the thirteen-year-old title character lives with her father, traveling from place to place, believing that her mother has been dead for ten years. Eventually, she discovers that her mother is alive; in fact, Terri has been kidnapped by her father. *After the Rain* provides a gentler mystery as fifteen-year-old Rachel gets to know her cranky grandfather before his death in a story that exemplifies Mazer's most recurring theme: the meaning of ordinary moments.

p.10

p.72

– Lisa Rowe Fraustino

Nicholasa Mohr

Born: November 1, 1935; New York, New York

voices.cla.umn.edu/newsite/authors/
MOHRnicholasa.htm

Nicholasa Mohr's fiction is set within New York's Puerto Rican communities, where poverty, prejudice, teenage pregnancy, drug addiction, violence, and crime are everyday realities. Although she does not ignore these hard truths, Mohr stresses the positive influence of family and community on her young women characters.

Mohr was born Nicholasa Golpe, the youngest of seven children and the only daughter of immigrants to New York from **Puerto Rico**. When Nicholasa was only eight, her father died, leaving his wife to provide for the family until she, too, died. Nicholasa's escape was always through art. After studying fashion design in trade school, she attended the Art Students' League in New York City. A trip to Mexico City, where she saw the work of such Mexican artists as muralist **Diego Rivera**, awakened her to social issues and also to the richness of her own Latino heritage.

After returning to New York, Nicholasa enrolled in the **New School for Social Research**. There she met Irwin Mohr, a graduate student in psychology. They were married and had two sons. Irwin died in 1978.

After Mohr put on a successful art exhibition in an East Side gallery, her art agent persuaded her to write a brief memoir. It later became the basis for Mohr's award-winning

.519
.482
p.305

TITLES

In Nueva York, 1977

Going Home, 1986

novel *Nilda* (1973). Two years later, Mohr published a collection of short fiction, *El Bronx Remembered* (1975). Although both works attracted young adult readers, Mohr has always insisted that she does not target any particular audience but writes for young and old alike.

Mohr also wrote *In Nueva York* as short fiction. However, the stories' single setting and use of recurring characters give the book the unity of a novel. Old and young characters wander in and out of Rudi's restaurant on New York's lower East Side, looking for love and losing it, looking for a long-lost mother and finding her, surviving a robbery, and talking about their problems in vivid language that captures the vibrant spirit of their neighborhood.

Felita, which Mohr published in 1979, is considered a children's book because its first-person narrator is an eight-year-old girl. However, in that book's sequel *Going Home*, Felita is eleven years old. She has a boyfriend and resents being deprived of her freedom by the protective males in her family. When Felita goes to Puerto Rico to spend a summer with relatives, she dis-

Diego Rivera

Diego Rivera was a famous twentieth century Mexican artist. He left Mexico for Europe in 1907 and was influenced not only by European artistic movements but also by political events. He was strongly influenced by the Russian revolution and after returning to Mexico in 1921, he joined the Communist Party. He married the Mexican artist Frida Kahlo, with whom he shared revolutionary views. He became known for his murals and their political content. In 1933 he was commissioned to install a mural in the lobby of the Rockefeller Center in New York City. A dispute over the depiction of Lenin resulted in the mural being destroyed in 1934. Rivera is known not only for his political views but also for reviving the pre-Columbus Mexican motifs in his art. His art gave Mexicans a pride in their artistic heritage independent of the European conquerers.

Nuyoricans

Puerto Ricans who live in New York City are nicknamed Nuyoricans. They have taken advantage of their identity to make many contributions to the arts in their new home. In 1973, Miguel Algarin, a professor, gathered poets in his living room to encourage their work. Soon they outgrew his apartment and moved their gatherings to a bar. Then, by 1980, they purchased a building. The Nuyorican Poets Café is now a thriving not-for-profit arts organization that encourages multicultural artists who often are underrepresented. They create poetry, music, hip hop, video, visual art, comedy, and theater.

483 covers the intense prejudice that islanders feel toward "Nuyoricans"—New York Puerto Ricans like herself. By the time Felita returns home, she has learned much about her roots but has also learned that prejudice can be found anywhere.

Although Nicholasa Mohr's works are centered in New York's Puerto Rican communities, they appeal to young women of all backgrounds who are coming to maturity in a rapidly changing world. Her books have won many awards; *In Nueva York*, for example, was cited by the p.45 **American Library Association** as a **Best Book for Young Adults**. In 1996 she received the **Lifetime Achievement Award** of the National Congress of Puerto Rican Woman. p.480 The following year she received the **Hispanic Heritage Award for Literature**. Mohr has also won awards for her nonfiction and has written a number of **radio** and television scripts. p.564 Her autobiography of her first fourteen years, *In My Own Words: Growing Up Inside the Sanctuary of My Imagination* (1995) was adapted for use in a 1997 television documentary.

— Rosemary M. Canfield Reisman

L. M. Montgomery

Born: November 30, 1874; Clifton (now New London),
    Prince Edward Island, Canada
Died: April 24, 1942; Toronto, Ontario, Canada
http://www.upei.ca/~/mmi

Lucy Maud Montgomery won fame as the creator of the eleven-year-old orphan girl who was the heroine of *Anne of Green Gables*. That book and its sequels continue to appeal to a broad range of readers, as do her other stories about re-markable girls and young women.

Born on Canada's remote **Prince Edward Island**, Montgomery herself had a lonely childhood. p.485 Her mother died when she was two. Soon afterward, her father moved to Saskatchewan, remarried, and started another family, leaving his daughter with her maternal grandparents in Cavendish, Prince Edward Island. Lucy's grandparents were strict and often punished her harshly. Since she dared not vent her anger, she coped with her situation by trying to find humor in it. She also took refuge in imagining herself in a different world. Out of these fantasies came her earliest poems and stories.

Montgomery decided to become a writer at an early age. Her works began appearing in periodicals when she was only sixteen. However, she also earned a teacher's license from Prince of Wales College in Charlottestown and later studied at Dalhousie College, in Halifax, Nova Scotia. After teaching on Prince Edward Island for three years, however, she resigned her position in order to help her widowed grandmother at home and to work in the Cavendish postoffice.

Montgomery's inspiration for *Anne of Green Ga-*

bles, the novel that made her famous, came from a newspaper story she saw about an orphanage that mistakenly sent a girl to work for an elderly couple who had requested a boy. Montgomery set her novel on Prince Edward Island. Her heroine, Anne Shirley, is a red-haired, eleven-year-old orphan with a hot temper. She has an aptitude for mischief but also has so kind a heart that she inspires love even in the elderly brother and sister caretakers who at first think her presence a mistake. *Anne of Green Gables* was an immediate success with both children and adults alike. No less a personage than Mark Twain called Anne his favorite child in all of fiction.

At her publisher's request, Montgomery wrote a sequel, *Anne of Avonlea*, in which her heroine, now sixteen, becomes the new schoolteacher in her community. In later books, Anne goes to college, marries, and has children. *Rilla of Ingleside* focuses on Anne's high-spirited youngest daughter.

In 1911, at the age of thirty-seven, Montgomery married the Reverend Ewen Macdonald, a Presbyterian minister, and settled down at Leaskdale, On-

Prince Edward Island

Prince Edward Island (PEI) is the smallest province in Canada. It is located on the east coast of Canada in the Gulf of St. Lawrence, just north of New Brunswick and Nova Scotia. Although largely rural, it is the most densely populated Canadian province. The areas around the capital, Charlottetown, are urbanized, and the majority of the island's inhabitants are descendants of immigrants from the British Isles. PEI is known for its red soil and rich farmland. Potatoes grown here are as well known in Canada as Idaho potatoes are in the U.S. The Dominion of Canada was formed in 1867 in Charlottetown. It is the setting of *Anne of Green Gables*.

tario. They had two sons and lost another at birth. While at Leaskdale, Montgomery began writing her trilogy about Emily Starr, another orphan. These books are Montgomery's most closely autobiographical works.

In 1925 L. M. Montgomery's husband accepted a call to Norval, Ontario. However, after a nervous breakdown, he retired, and the family moved to Toronto, Ontario. Montgomery died in 1942, but her stories of girls and young women who refuse to be defeated by circumstances remain as popular as when p.486 they first appeared. *Anne of Green Gables* and the other Anne stories have been translated into sixty languages and have also been adapted for film, stage, and television. In recognition of her contributions to literature, she was awarded **Order of the British Empire** in 1935.

– Rosemary M. Canfield Reisman

Anne of Green Gables, the Movies

A charming adaptation of *Anne of Green Gables* was released on screen by RKO Pictures in 1934. It was notable for the beauty of the Canadian locations. More recently, Kevin Sullivan produced an *Anne of Green Gables* series that was first broadcast on Canadian television. The first part, broadcast in 1985, was a very faithful adaptation of the book and enjoyed great popularity. Part two, *Anne of Avonlea* (1987), deviated somewhat from the book but still satisfied fans. The third part, *Anne of Green Gables: The Continuing Story* (2000), disappointed many fans. They felt that it was not true to the story and that Anne was just not Anne. Sullivan also produced an animated version that was broadcast on PBS in the U.S. in 2001. *Anne of Green Gables, The Musical*, is produced at Charlottetown's Festival and is the longest running musical in Canada.

An Na
Born: 1972; Korea

With her first novel, *A Step from Heaven*, Korean American writer **An Na** powerfully established herself as an author of moving and relevant fiction for young adults. Her first book successfully combines the adventures of a girl's life from four to eighteen with a naturally flowing reflection on the challenges of growing up. She deals with a less-than-ideal father, sibling rivalry, feeling different from anybody else, and learning to survive in a new environment. Organized in short chapters, the story of Young Ju Park is full of discoveries about her, her family, and her new life in America.

An Na was born in Korea, from which she emigrated with her family to America when she was still a little girl. She spent her teenage years in San Diego, California and quietly excelled at school. Pushed hard by her strict parents, she did not socialize there. Only at Korean Church did she feel she could have fun with her best friends. Her experiences clearly influenced some of the characters and events in *A Step from Heaven*.

Na loves reading, and as a child told stories to her brother and sister through her stuffed animals. After she graduated from Amherst College in Massachusetts, she started to teach middle school then earned a master of fine arts degree in writing children's literature from **Norwich University** in Vermont. After *A Step from Heaven* was published, she and her husband, James, went trekking in the **Himalayas**. In an Internet café in Nepal, they learned that her book had become a finalist for the **National**

p.611

489

TITLE

A Step from Heaven, 2001

Michael L. Printz Award

Each year, the Michael L. Printz Award names a young adult book for its outstanding literary excellence. The award honors Printz, a school librarian from Topeka, Kansas, who made finding the right book for each reader his mission. He was active in the Young Adult Librarian Services Association (YALSA), a division of the American Library Association (ALA) that provides the committee that selects the winning book. The award is given annually to books published the previous year and identified by their publishers as young adult literature. In addition to the award winner, the committee also can name up to four Honor Books. The nominated books can be fiction, nonfiction, poetry, or an anthology. The award is sponsored by the ALA journal *Booklist*.

p.122 Book Award for 2001. In 2002, when Na was no longer a teacher, she alternated her residences between Oakland, California, and Warren, Vermont, while continuing to write.

A Step from Heaven follows Young Ju Park from the time she leaves Korea as a preschool girl who gets her straight hair permed for the occasion. She arrives in America, where her family hopes for a better life. However, things do not go as smoothly as anticipated, and her parents run into personal and economic problems. As her uncle tells her, America is not quite heaven, but is a step away from it.

After Young Ju's baby brother, Joon Ho, is born, her father shifts all attention to him. Hurt, Young Ju has to cope with this and other rifts in her family. When her father's mother dies, and he fails at work, he starts drinking too much and becomes abusive again toward his wife. Terrified, Young Ju has to struggle with a bad family situation and her father's aversion toward her European American girlfriend, Amanda. However, her inner strength carries her through, and she readies herself for college.

An Na's first novel has captured both female and male readers and the critics. It won the Mi-chael L. Printz Award from the Young Adult Li-

p.488

p.45

.480

.101

brary Services Association and the American Library Association's Best Books for Young Adults award. Na's authentic characters and her personal storytelling go far beyond stereotypes. Even Young Ju's alcoholic father comes across as a real character, and her brother Joon Ho must deal with restrictively high expectations. Na's narration is intense, thoughtful, and fully leads readers into the world of her protagonist.

.233

– R. C. Lutz

Himalayas

The Himalayas are the the highest mountain range in the world, with more than forty peaks higher than 22,865 feet. There are actually three parallel ranges, the Greater, the Lesser, and the Outer Himalayas. The Greater Himalayas have the highest elevations among the three ranges, and the highest mountain on earth, Mount Everest (29,035 feet), is found there. The Himalayan mountain system is geologically young and subject to severe earthquakes. Extensive tourism is common throughout the ranges. The Himalayas are shared geographically by India, Pakistan, and Nepal.

AN NA

Beverley Naidoo

Born: May 21, 1943; Johannesburg, South Africa

www.beverleynaidoo.com/index2.html

p.150

p.491

Beverley Naidoo's adolescent characters give readers intimate and often disturbing insights into the politics of racial hatred under South Africa's former **apartheid** system. Born to a middle-class white family in **Johannesburg**, South Africa, Naidoo attended an all-white school. She later described the experience as being similar to "being brought up to be a horse with blinkers." Eventually, however, she met people who challenged her. She removed the blinkers and began to feel angry about the terrible things of which she could see that she was part.

In 1967 she moved to England. While teaching in London, she found a shortage of educational materials to use in teaching children about South African apartheid. At the request of the Education Group of the British Defense and Aid Fund for Southern Africa, she wrote *Journey to Jo'burg* and a nonfiction work, *Censoring Reality: An Examination of Books on South Africa* (1985). Soon after their publication, both books were banned in Naidoo's homeland.

Journey to Jo'burg tells of two black children, Naledi and Tiro, who live in a South African village. Because their younger sister is dying, they decide to travel 150 miles to Johannesburg to find their mother. They go the only way they can, on foot. Through Naledi's eyes, the poli-

Johannesburg

Johannesburg is the largest city in South Africa and the hub of South Africa's commercial, financial, industrial, and mining activities. It has a population of some three million people. Located more than a mile above sea level, it enjoys warm summers and cold to mild winters. In 1886, the discovery of gold triggered one the of biggest gold rushes in the history of the world. Johannesburg is also called *Egoli*, a native Zulu name meaning "City of Gold."

tics of South Africa unfold for the reader. In the sequel, *Chains of Fire*, Naledi and Tiro face forced removal from their village to a new "homeland" of stark iron huts and barren soil. When Naledi organizes a student protest, her efforts are met with police brutality. Tiro goes missing, and apartheid threatens to crush both the people and their spirit.

In *No Turning Back*, twelve-year-old Sipho runs away from a violent stepfather to seek his fate as a **homeless** street child in Johannesburg. There, learning to survive, he experiences the realities of both trust and betrayal as South Africa approaches its first nonracial elections during the early 1990's.

The Other Side of Truth tells the story of twelve-year-old Sade Solaja and her younger brother Femi. After Sade witnesses her mother's murder, she and Femi realize that the soldiers are out to kill their father, an outspoken Nigerian journalist. They flee their country and reach England as refugees, but their troubles have only begun.

Beverley Naidoo has won many awards for her books. *Journey to Jo'burg* was a **Parents' Choice Honor Book** for Paperback Literature of the Parents' Choice Foundation in 1988. *Chain of Fire* won

African Studies Association Children's Africana Book Award

The African Studies Association was founded in 1957 to bring people with scholarly and professional interest in Africa together. The Association publishes and distributes materials on Africa and provides services to schools, business, the media, and the community about Africa. The Children's Africana Book Awards were started in 1991 and are given annually in two categories: Books for Young Children and Books for Older Readers. The award is given to a nominated book that was published the previous year by an American publisher. The award encourages the publication of accurate and balanced books on Africa.

p.480

Best Books for Young Adults honors from the American Library Association in 1991. *No Turning Back* received the **African Studies Association's Children's Book Award** for Older Readers in 1998 and was an International Reading Association Teachers' Choice that same year. *The Other Side of Truth* won the **Carnegie Medal** of the Library Association in the United Kingdom in 2000. It was *Booklist*'s 2001 **Top of the List Winner** for Youth Fiction.

p.492

p.62

p.143

– Faith Hickman Brynie

Donna Jo Napoli

Born: February 28, 1948; Miami, Florida

www.donnajonapoli.com

p.117
p.87

Donna Jo Napoli is best known for her innovative retellings of classic myths and fairy tales, but she also writes **historical fiction** and **fantasy**. She often uses the first-person voice and present-tense verbs to give intimacy and immediacy to her narratives. In many of her books, she explores the twists and turns of loving relationships—often of children with their parents—probing the reasons that underlie human behavior.

The daughter of a gambler father subject to severe mood swings and a mother prone to magical thinking, Napoli grew up with a sense of instability that has helped her get inside her characters, whose own situations are often unstable. Raised in the Roman Catholic faith and educated in both mathematics and linguistics, Napoli often writes about how different religions influence people's daily decisions. For example, *Beast* is the "Beauty and the Beast" folktale retold from the Beast's point of view. Drawing her inspiration from an old **Charles Lamb** poem, Napoli sets her version in Persia instead of France, and the ancient Islamic faith plays a pivotal role in the story. Napoli believes that people are products of their culture, even if they rebel against it.

494

Napoli was influenced helpfully by a high school Latin teacher who encouraged her to scrutinize the psychological underpinnings of time-honored myths and legends, which a number of her books do. For example, *The Magic Circle* retells the story of Hansel and Gretel from the witch's point of view, and *Crazy Jack* is the traditional tale of Jack and the Bean-

stalk told in a way that analyzes motivations. *Spinner* is a retelling of the Rumpelstiltskin tale, with life stories invented for the miller's daughter and the spinner who helps her. Set in Switzerland in the mid-sixteenth century, *Zel* is the Rapunzel story told from the points of view of the mother, the girl, and the young nobleman who loves her. *Sirena* is an amalgam of romantic fantasy and classical legend. It tells of a mermaid in the time of the Trojan War made immortal by the love of a shipwrecked soldier. p.495

Some of Napoli's books are historical fiction. *Song of the Magdalene* is set in the Holy Land of Christ's time. It tells of Mary Magdalene's life as the daughter of a wealthy Jewish widower and a follower of Jesus Christ. In *Daughter of Venice*, set in 1592, fourteen-year-old Donata Mocenigo, daughter of a noble family, faces seclusion in a convent. She disguises herself as a boy in order to explore the city and get an education. p.506

Napoli uses twentieth century Venice as a setting for *Stones in Water* and *For the Love of Venice*. Inspired by the wartime experiences of one of Napo-

Charles Lamb

Charles Lamb was an English poet and essayist who was born in 1775 and died in 1834. He was a friend of the great English Romantic poets Samuel Taylor Coleridge, William Wordsworth, and Robert Southey. His essays, first published in *London Magazine* and collected as *Essays of Elia*, continue to be considered masterpieces for capturing in prose the spirit of the Romantic poets. His life was plagued by a strain of mental illness in his family. He once committed himself to Hoxton Asylum for six weeks. More seriously, his older sister killed their mother with a kitchen knife. She was tried, found insane, and released to Lamb's custody. They became inseparable except during her periods of madness when Lamb would commit her to Hoxton Asylum until her spell had passed.

Trojan War

In the *Iliad*, Homer, hailed as the father of poetry, tells the story of the Trojan War. Helen, the wife of King Menelaus of Sparta, was abducted by her lover Paris and taken to the walled city of Troy. Agamemnon, Menelaus's brother, gathers the Greek tribes and camps outside Troy for ten years before moving into battle. Achilles, a mortal son of the gods, withdraws from the war over differences with Agamemnon. When the Trojans defeat the Greeks, Achilles reenters the battle to avenge the death of his friend Patroclus at the hand of Hector, son of the Trojan king. Achilles kills Hector and takes his body to the Greek ships. King Priam begs for the return of Hector's body, and the gods ask Achilles to return the body of the Trojan warrior to his people. Achilles complies and

a twelve-day truce is called so that each side can bury and mourn their dead. This complex story seems all the more unusual because of the interference of the Greek gods in mortal matters.

li's friends, *Stones in Water* is the story of two Italian boys seized by German soldiers and sent to endure hard labor, brutal weather conditions, and near starvation in a work camp. *For the Love of Venice* is a romance with a political message. In it, seventeen-year-old Percy meets Graziella, a beautiful Venetian girl who wants to save her city from the thoughtless actions of tourists.

Donna Jo Napoli has won numerous awards for her books. *The Magic Circle* received a *Booklist* **Editor's Choice Award** and an **American Library Association Best Books for Young Adults** award. *Stones in Water* won the **Golden Kite Award** and the **Sydney Taylor Book Award** of the National Association of Jewish Libraries. *Beast* was a *School Library Journal* **Best Book**.

— Faith Hickman Brynie

p.143
p.480
p.111
p.195
p.45
p.408

Joan Lowery Nixon

Born: February 3, 1927; Los Angeles, California
Died: July 5, 2003; Houston, Texas

www.teenreads.com/authors/au-nixon-joan-
   lowery.asp

Joan Lowery Nixon is best known as a writer of mystery books that combine personal problems with mysteries that must be solved. She has written the Orphan Train series, the Hollywood Daughters series, and the **Ellis Island** series.

p.498

Born in Los Angeles, Nixon attended **Hollywood High School** and had many famous neighbors, including the legendary film director Cecil B. DeMille and comedian W. C. Fields. She later attended the University of Southern California, where she majored in journalism and earned a teaching credential. She then taught kindergarten and first grade in Los Angeles. She wanted to write from an early age; she published her first poem when she was only ten and her first article at seventeen. She had a long career, publishing her first book in 1964 and one hundredth in 1994.

p.497

Nixon earned her reputation writing mysteries, which she considers one of her favorite pursuits. In *The Other Side of Dark*, a seventeen-year-old girl awakens from a four-year coma to hunt down the man who murdered her mother and put her in the coma. The girl not only must deal with adjusting to life after being in a coma but also must resolve the mystery of her mother's death. After a girl nearly dies in a swimming accident in *Whispers from the Dead*, her family moves to Texas, and she feels as if she is being watched. She discovers that a murder once took place in her new house and determines to find out what is haunting her. In *The Kidnapping of Christina Lattimore* the teenage heroine is kidnapped from her driveway and held for ransom. After she is freed, she is accused of plotting her own kidnapping in order to extort money from her grandmother and must prove her innocence. In *The Ghosts of Now*, a high school senior investigates the hit-and-run accident that put her brother in a coma.

In 1987 Nixon took a break from mysteries to begin the Orphan Train series, which includes such books as *A Place to Belong* and *A Family Apart*. These books investigate a relatively unknown aspect of American history beginning in 1854 when more than 100,000 **homeless** children were taken from the streets of New York City and sent by trains to new homes in the Midwest and the West. Nixon studied letters and journals from the era and felt that she had to tell the forgotten stories of these children's lives. She also created another series dealing with American history, the Ellis Island novels, *Land of Hope*, *Land of Praise*, and *Land of Dreams*, which

Hollywood High

Located at the corner of Sunset Boulevard and Highland Avenue in Hollywood, California, Hollywood High was once the school of choice for the children of the movie industry. Following the school's founding in 1910, the movie industry made Hollywood home and flourished. Such notable movie and television figures as Carol Burnett, Judy Garland, Lana Turner, James Garner, Ione Skye, and Rita Wilson were students at Hollywood High. An Alumni Museum is housed in the school library and displays photos of stars as well as donated memorabilia, such as letterman jackets, awards, and school yearbooks. Today, Hollywood High has an enrollment of some 2,700 students of diverse ethnic background.

follow three teenagers immigrating to the United States from Russia, Ireland and Sweden during the 1880's. Her third series, Hollywood Daughters, which includes *Overnight Sensation*, is a trilogy about a family living in Hollywood over a period of fifty years; it is partly based on her own childhood memories.

p.72 Joan Lowery Nixon was a four-time recipient of the **Edgar Allan Poe Award** for Best Juvenile Mystery. She also received two **Spur Awards** from p.33 the Western Writers of America and the **California Young Reader Medal**. In 1997 she served as the president of the Mystery Writers of America.

– Mary Virginia Davis

Ellis Island

Located in New York Harbor, Ellis Island was once the gateway to America for more than twelve million immigrants. Opened as an immigration clearing center in 1892, it saw thousands pass through its doors each day. They were checked for disease and disability before being allowed to enter the U.S. Restrictions on immigration in the 1920's decreased the flow; by 1954 Ellis Island was closed. Over time, the abandoned buildings began to deteriorate. They were made part of the Statue of Liberty National Park in 1965. Funds were eventually raised to renovate the old main building and in 1990 it reopened as the Ellis Island Immigration Museum.

Photo Credits

Subject Index

Oxford University, 173
premed program, 656
Rhodes Scholarship, 47
Rugby School, 599
scholarships, 380
School Library Journal, 195
School of Librarianship, 134
Smith College, 398
South Carolina Association of School Librarians, 378
University of North Carolina at Chapel Hill, 194
Yeshiva University, 278
Eight Mules from Monterey (Beatty), 62
El Bronx Remembered (Mohr), 482
Elidor (Garner), 268
Elizabethan England, 311
Ella Enchanted (Levine), 403
Elliott cousin series (Thesman), 674
Ellis Island, 498
Ellis Island series (Nixon), 497
Elm Street Lot, The (Pearce), 536
Elske (Voigt), 695
Emma (Austen), 33
Emma Tupper's Diary (Dickinson), 200
Emperor's Winding Sheet, The (Paton Walsh), 529
Empty Sleeve, The (Garfield), 266
Engineer, computer, 705
England Have My Bones (T. White), 715
English class system, 32
Ennead, The (Mark), 457
Enough Is Too Much Already (Mark), 458
Epistolary novel, 441
Erie Canal, 221
Errands (Guest), 293
Escape from Egypt (Levitin), 407
Eskimos, 534
ESP. *See* Extrasensory perception
Ethics, 10
Ethiopia, 77
Ethnic Boston, 434
Eton College, 200
Eva (Dickinson), 200
Everard's Ride (Jones), 362
Everett Anderson's Christmas Coming (Clifton), 137
Everett Anderson's Goodbye (Clifton), 137
Every Time a Rainbow Dies (Williams-Garcia), 723

Everywhere (B. Brooks), 102
Examination, The (Bosse), 84
Extra Innings (Robert Peck), 542
Extrasensory perception, 306, 444. *See also* Telepathy
Extreme Elvin (Lynch), 434
Eyes of Kid Midas, The (Shusterman), 623
Eyes of the Amaryllis, The (Babbitt), 38

Face in Every Window, A (Nolan), 501
Face on the Milk Carton, The (Cooney), 154
Faces of Fear, The (Hughes), 351
Facts Speak for Themselves, The (Cole), 143
Fade (Cormier), 161
Faery Lands of the South Seas (Nordhoff and Hall), 503
Fahrenheit 451 (Bradbury), 92
Fahrenheit 451, the movie, 93
Faith healer, 678
  and *curandera*, 678
Falkland Islands War, 458
Fall Secrets (Boyd), 89
Family Album series (Hoobler), 346
Family Apart, A (Nixon), 497
Family Footlights (Barne), 40
Fantasy literature, 87
  Adams, Richard, 7
  Alexander, Lloyd, 16
  Barron, T. A., 46
  Boston, L. M., 85
  Bradbury, Ray, 91
  Brooks, Terry, 103
  Cooper, Susan, 157
  Cresswell, Helen, 169
  Dickinson, Peter, 199
  Farmer, Nancy, 223
  Gaiman, Neil, 256
  Garfield, Leon, 265
  Hahn, Mary Downing, 301
  Hamilton, Virginia, 304
  Haskins, James S., 313
  Hillerman, Tony, 334
  Hughes, Monica, 349
  Hunter, Mollie, 352
  Jones, Diana Wynne, 361
  Kemp, Gene, 364
  Klause, Annette Curtis, 376
  Le Guin, Ursula, 394
  L'Engle, Madeleine, 397